LOST RAILWAYS OF BERKSHIRE

Rupert Matthews

COUNTRYSIDE BOOKS
NEWBURY BERKSHIRE

First published 2006
© Rupert Matthews 2006

COUNTRYSIDE BOOKS
3 Catherine Road
Newbury, Berkshire

To view our complete range of books,
please visit us at
www.countrysidebooks.co.uk

ISBN 1 85306 990 6
EAN 978 185306 990 1

Cover picture of the 13.25 Paddington to Kingswear
train passing through Newbury, headed by
6009 King Charles II in the summer of 1957
is from an original painting by
Colin Doggett

Designed by Peter Davies, Nautilus Design

Produced through MRM Associates Ltd., Reading
Typeset by CJWT Solutions, Newton-le-Willows
Printed in Spain

CONTENTS

ABBREVIATIONS

The following abbreviations are used in this book:

BR	British Rail
DMU	Diesel motor unit
DN&SR	Didcot, Newbury and Southampton Railway
GWR	Great Western Railway
ILVR	Independent Lambourn Valley Railway
LSWR	London and South Western Railway
SER	South Eastern Railway
SWWJR	Staines, Wokingham and Woking Junction Railway

ACKNOWLEDGEMENTS

I would like to thank the volunteers of the Cholsey and Wallingford Railway Preservation Society for their kindness and support. I would also like to thank the Didcot Railway Centre, which has a magnificent array of railway lines, rolling stock and buildings on show. This is run by the volunteers of the Great Western Society. Details of how to join the Society and how to visit Didcot Railway Centre are available from Great Western Society, Didcot Railway Centre, Didcot, OX11 7NJ. Telephone: 01235 817200; email: didrlyc@globalnet.co.uk; www.didcotrailwaycentre.org.uk. I am also grateful to those who have allowed me to use their photos, each of which is credited accordingly. Illustrations without a credit are from my own collections. Finally I must thank the people of Berkshire for the warm welcome I received while researching this book and for their tolerance of a man poking about abandoned railway lines.

A Collett 48xx 0-4-2 tank engine runs along the line at the Didcot Railway Centre. Engines such as these were common sights on the lost railways of Berkshire. (Courtesy of the Didcot Railway Centre)

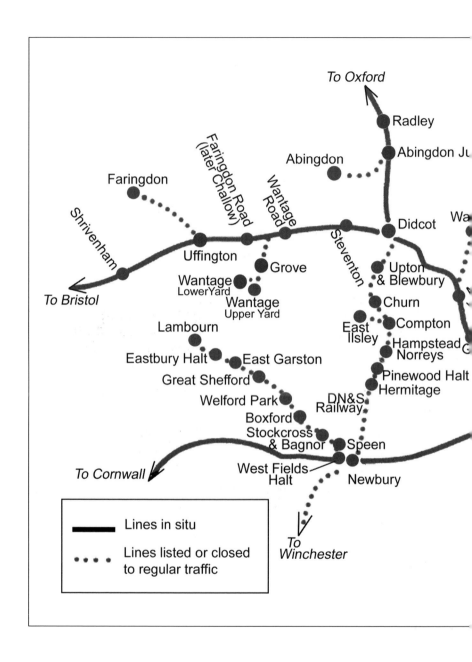

To Oxford

Radley

Abingdon Ju

Abingdon

Faringdon Road (later Challow)

Wantage Road

Faringdon

Didcot

Wa

Shrivenham

Steventon

Uffington

Grove

Upton & Blewbury

Wantage Lower Yard

Churn

To Bristol

Wantage Upper Yard

Compton

East Ilsley

Lambourn

Hampstead Norreys

G

Eastbury Halt

East Garston

Pinewood Halt

Great Shefford

Hermitage

Welford Park

DN&S Railway

Boxford

Stockcross & Bagnor

Speen

West Fields Halt

Newbury

To Cornwall

Lines in situ

Lines listed or closed to regular traffic

To Winchester

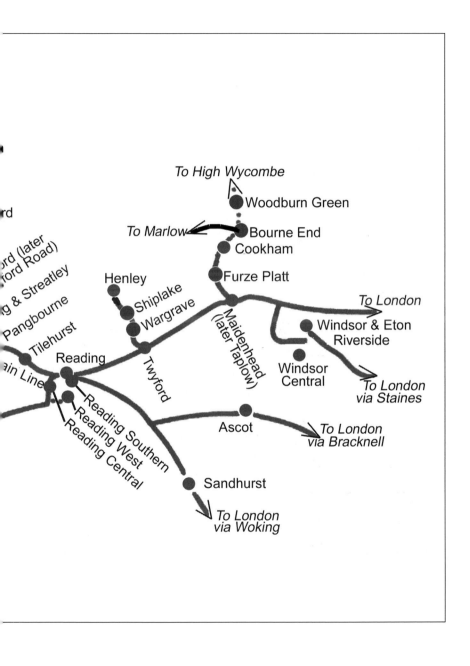

Introduction

There is something evocatively romantic about lost railways. Now overgrown and disused, these were once the main arteries of life in the rural areas of Berkshire. Businesses relied on the little tank engines puffing back and forth along the short branch lines, while passengers travelled to work, to visit friends or to court their sweethearts.

But it was not simply romance that drove the railways over the downs and along the valleys of Berkshire. It was cold financial sense as well. When the quickest alternative was a good horse, the railways offered fast, safe and cheap transport for people and goods. Towns made their fortunes by being on the railway, Reading leapt from being a second rate market town to being the biggest town in Berkshire within two decades of the railway arriving in 1840.

And the railways transformed the way people lived their lives. No longer were families forced to live crammed up against the dirty factories that provided work. Commuting allowed Berkshire citizens to live in pleasant suburbs or villages and then travel to their place of employment. Nor was it any longer necessary to subsist on the bread baked from local grain or on meat from local livestock. The speedy railways brought fresh fish from the coast, delicacies from specialist market gardeners and all manner of new and exciting food.

The railways made Berkshire the place it is today. But it could not last. By the middle of the 20th century, the competition from road transport and the sheer convenience of the private motor car spelled the end for all but the most profitable lines. One by one the old branch lines closed down. The tracks were torn up, the stations converted to other uses and the bridges taken down for safety reasons. Gradually they faded from view as redevelopment swallowed the old sites, and re-growth of trees and brambles, quite literally, covered their tracks.

And yet all is not quite gone. Here and there remnants remain. It is possible to trace the routes of the old lines through the

The sad end that came to all too many engines and rolling stock from the lost railways of Berkshire was the scrap yard. These old coaches have been partially dismantled, but are in fact destined for renovation. (Courtesy of the Didcot Railway Centre)

beautiful Berkshire countryside, into villages and through towns. Sometimes there is only the name of a street to show where a station once stood. Elsewhere a public path runs along a deep cutting or over a towering embankment where once trains steamed their way.

This book explores the stories behind the lost railways of Berkshire and attempts to seek out what vestiges have been left behind.

Rupert Matthews

9

1
God's Wonderful Railway

The Great Western

A goods train is hauled out of Didcot by a 2-4-0 tender locomotive in August 1931. The tender proudly bears the words 'Great Western'.

Of all the lost railways of Berkshire none was so magnificent in conception or design as the original Great Western Railway, so prestigious and impressive that it soon acquired the nickname of 'God's Wonderful Railway'. Although the GWR was to survive, it did so only in greatly modified form and function. That which remains is still impressive, but is merely a shadow of the original vision that drove the company on.

The GWR was born in Bristol in the autumn of 1832 when a group of merchants in the city got together to discuss their

10

The coat of arms of the Great Western Railway, the company that originally ran most of the Lost Railways of Berkshire.

transport problems. These were considerable. Bristol was a major port for the Atlantic trade with hundreds of ships each year putting in to unload cargoes for distribution throughout southern England, or to pick up cargoes for export over the world's oceans to the British Empire. To make their money, the merchants had to be able to guarantee that the goods could move across the country with speed and reliability. That was where the problems set in.

The bulk of the goods that landed at Bristol went east to London and southern England by means of barges that were pulled by horses up the Avon to Bath, then along the Kennet and Avon Canal to Reading, thence down the Thames to London. Unfortunately the Avon was notoriously prone to floods in autumn and the canal was often closed in winter when the water froze. Meanwhile the Thames was liable to run so low in the summer that the barges grounded on the shallower sections. A journey that in theory lasted a week could often stretch out for more than a month. The only alternative was to transfer goods from barge to cart, but carters often charged three times as much as the bargemen.

One of the Bristol merchants, sadly history does not record which one, brought to the meeting the second Annual Report of the Liverpool and Manchester Railways Company. The report stated, with numerous charts and tabulations, that the railway moved goods twice as fast as the swiftest cart but cost only half as much as moving goods by canal. The merchants were quickly convinced that what they needed was a railway from Bristol to London. A committee of senior merchants was set up to investigate the matter.

The committee did not delay for long. In March 1833 they hired a promising 26 year old engineer who was in Bristol at the time designing a bridge over the Avon at Clifton. His name was Isambard Kingdom Brunel, and he was destined to become the greatest engineer Britain has ever produced. Brunel gathered together a team of surveyors and quickly set about finding a route suitable for a railway.

On 30 July Brunel was back in Bristol to speak to a public meeting at the Guildhall. He had maps showing several different route options to cover the 120 miles to London and detailed costings that priced the enterprise at the then staggering amount of £2,805,330. The packed meeting applauded Brunel's work, then passed a motion to set up a company to be called the Great Western Railway Company – later universally termed the GWR. There would be a sale of 30,000 shares at £100 each – a price that effectively meant that only relatively wealthy men could afford to buy them.

Building a railway required an Act of Parliament to give the company authority to purchase land for the line, undertake engineering works and to realign roads or paths affected by the construction of the railway. Before a Bill could be introduced to Parliament, detailed surveys of the actual route needed to be undertaken, drawings of all the principal bridges, embankments, cuttings and stations produced and all the details finalised. Brunel was given the job.

At first Brunel began designing a perfectly straightforward rail system, adopting the basic pattern that had been established by George Stephenson in 1812 at Killingworth Colliery in Northumberland. This saw wooden trucks mounted on unsprung metal carriages, which rode on wheels with a gauge of 4 feet 8½ inches. This gauge had been in existence since Roman times and was equally convenient for a road vehicle whether drawn by a single horse or by two working together, and so had been chosen for the original horse-drawn Killingworth railway.

Brunel, however, did not have old colliery wagons to reuse nor an existing track to adapt. He was working from scratch and as he progressed he began to question both the gauge and the method of track building that had been perfected by Stephenson and adapted by subsequent railway engineers.

At the core of Brunel's doubts was his vision of what railways could achieve. Stephenson had been concerned with moving trucks of coal a few miles from colliery to port. Even the hugely successful Liverpool to Manchester railway that had inspired the GWR had the sole purpose of linking the industrial town of Manchester to its principal port at Liverpool. But Brunel was building a much larger railway that not only took in major cities, but also numerous towns along the way. And, as he worked, other entrepreneurs and engineers approached him with schemes to link the GWR by rail to other towns as far west as Cornwall as well as to the north and south.

Brunel began to envisage a whole network of railways connecting the main towns and cities of England, as well as having stopping points for villages and smaller towns. It was no longer just a matter of taking goods from dock to market along routes previously run by carts or barges; he began to see the great possibilities of a rail network. Fresh milk, eggs and other crops could be conveyed from the country to distant towns, providing a cheap, healthy diet for town-dwellers and a new market for farmers. Passengers could travel back and forth more readily than on horse-drawn coaches, enabling families to meet more often and men to find work a distance from their homes.

The whole lifestyle of the nation could be transformed. Speed and capacity would be the keys to success.

With this in mind, Brunel looked again at the basic railway pattern established by Stephenson. With a wider wheelbase, he realised, the centre of gravity could be brought down lower, making the trains more stable and thus safer at high speeds. A wider gauge would also allow much of the mechanics to be placed beside, rather than underneath, the engines and wagons, which would lower the profile of the trains, cutting air resistance. This in turn would enable the use of larger wheels, which would reduce friction.

Of course, a wider gauge had disadvantages. Any bridges or cuttings would have to be made wider, making them more expensive to build. It would also be impossible to turn corners as sharply as did trains on a standard gauge, so the route of the railway would have to include only wide sweeping curves. Taking both advantages and disadvantages into account, however, Brunel decided that a gauge of 7 feet ¼ inch was perfect. The GWR was to be built to the broad gauge.

Not content with designing the railway itself, Brunel also set to work designing the stations. That at Pangbourne, to the west of Reading, is a particularly fine example.

Generally the towns where stations were to be built approved of the railway. Their councils and leading citizens lobbied Parliament in favour of the GWR Bill in eager anticipation of the commercial advantages they would gain.

The rural districts and landowners tended to oppose the railway. Many farms and estates were to be cut in two by the building of the rail line. The men working the land were accustomed to being able to walk from any part of their farms to any other or to drive livestock about without any hindrance. But the GWR was proposing to install footbridges or tunnels at only infrequent intervals. This would make life difficult for farmers and might reduce the value of the land. There were also various horror stories circulating about sheep that had dropped dead of fright when a steam engine blew its whistle and of horses suddenly bolting, causing injury to riders or passengers in carriages. The people affected in this way were not even to gain a local station for their use. It must be remembered that steam trains at this date were the largest, noisiest and dirtiest machines that had ever been seen. It was little wonder that many people did not want them near their homes.

As might be expected the canal company, bargemen, coach companies and the Thames Commissioners all opposed the GWR because it was bound to take trade away from them. These men and organisations had deep pockets and much influence in society. Combined with the wealthy landowners, in Berkshire as elsewhere, they had considerable clout.

At the end of July 1834 the House of Lords voted down the GWR Bill.

But neither the Bristol merchants nor Brunel were to be denied. Brunel altered his plans to appease the less entrenched opposition, while the merchants worked hard to depict the more obdurate opposition as being motivated by selfish interests while the GWR wanted only what was good for Britain. In February 1835 the revised GWR Bill was introduced to Parliament. On 30 August it was passed. Next day the *Reading Mercury* had the lead headline 'The Passing of the Great Western Railway Bill' and devoted much of its news coverage to the event.

The line from London to Maidenhead was completed quickly, with the first train running along the stretch of line on 31 May 1838. But pushing the GWR west through the rest of Berkshire was to prove to be a major effort for Brunel.

The first obstacle was the Thames at Maidenhead, which was 100 yards wide. In order to show Parliament that it was willing to make concessions to opposition, the GWR had agreed to the demand of the Thames Commissioners that there should be only one bridge pier in the river, so that barges were not obstructed, and that the bridge should not obstruct the towpath. The Thames Commissioners gleefully predicted that these conditions would make it impossible to build a bridge at Maidenhead. They reckoned without the GWR's mastermind.

Brunel designed a bridge that had two enormously wide, flat brick arches. Nobody had ever before built arches so flat and many people, including a good number of professional engineers, thought the structure would collapse within weeks of being completed. The bridge was finished in May 1838 and the wooden supports that had held it up during construction were removed. Everyone held their breath. Three weeks later the eastern arch began to sag. Brunel hurriedly ordered the timber supports put back into place. He quickly realised that one of the contractors had not used the correct cement as bonding between the bricks. The offending section was removed and rebuilt.

Then the wooden supports were removed once again. This time the bridge stood solid. Even a violent storm, followed by a powerful flood in late January 1840 had no effect on the Maidenhead bridge, which then became something of a minor tourist attraction.

Meanwhile, Brunel had moved on to tackle the second great obstacle to the GWR in Berkshire: Sonning Hill. The section through the hill would require a cutting over two miles long and up to 60 feet deep. The hill was composed largely of gravel with bands of clay, neither of which was a particularly stable material.

The bridge that carries the GWR over the Thames at Maidenhead was for many years something of a tourist attraction. This postcard dates from 1909.

This postcard of 1908 shows the mighty Sonning Cutting, which took nearly four years to complete and cost the lives of four men.

The cutting was going to need more gently sloping sides than normal and would require buttressing in places, all of which increased the amount of work to be done. To accomplish this, Brunel had none of the mechanical diggers and bulldozers that make light work of such projects in the 21st century. He had only manpower to dig with and horse-drawn carts to take away the spoil.

The navvies who worked on the GWR project took their name from the navigators who had laboured on the canal construction projects of the previous century. These were tough men for they needed to be physically strong to wield the shovels and picks that shifted so many tons of soil and rock. The majority were young, unmarried men who had left their farms to spend a few years earning the good wages paid by the railways, before returning home to marry and settle down. A large proportion came from Ireland. As with any group of tough, rootless youths throughout history, the navvies often caused trouble. The prodigious thirst of men who had been working hard all day

17

and had good wages paid in silver coin jingling in their pockets made drinking a constant problem. It was not that the navvies were habitual criminals, it was just that they were young, boisterous men whose idea of a good time was considerably rougher than that of the good citizens whose villages they visited. When the navvies came to a district it was common practice for valuables to be deposited in banks and for the more impressionable young ladies to be sent to stay with relatives a safe distance away.

When the GWR announced that it was building a semi-permanent camp close to Reading for workers on the Sonning Cutting, the council of Reading was uneasy – and when it was realised that over 1,200 navvies would be in residence for four years, the townsfolk were aghast. The local newspapers were filled with articles by doom-mongers predicting ruin to Reading and its inhabitants.

In the summer of 1836 the navvies arrived. All too soon the much feared drunken brawls and high-spirited japes were taking their toll on the town of Reading. Trouble flared and friction between townsfolk and navvies became constant, but there were no really serious incidents. Then on 28 May 1838 the disaster long predicted by the more gloomy residents burst upon Reading in full force.

The contractor excavating part of the cutting ran into financial difficulties. For the second week running no wages were paid to the workmen. Hundreds of navvies threw down their tools and marched into Reading to confront the company officials at their offices. Next day the rest of the workforce also downed tools and streamed into the town to join the protest. The chief official of the defaulting company made the mistake of haranguing the angry navvies, ordering them back to work on threat of instant dismissal and no backpay. The foolish man was promptly set upon by an enraged gang, though he escaped serious injury by making himself scarce.

As the local police were clearly unable to contain the situation, the Mayor of Reading sent a constable riding at speed to Windsor to ask for assistance. His request was so alarming that it was passed to the military and a squadron of almost a hundred

Horse Guards rode out of Windsor, arriving in Reading before dusk fell. Resplendent in their blue coats and white breeches, the Horse Guards came clattering into Reading with sabres bouncing on their knees and carbines stowed on their saddles. Concerned that the arrival of a second group of aggressive young men might inflame the situation, the Mayor sent the soldiers to camp outside town and guard the railway works against sabotage.

Next day, the troopers stood guard in the cutting while the navvies roamed around town. Some were, by this time, penniless and begged food from townsfolk, who responded by handing out bread and biscuits in the town centre. Messages, meanwhile, were flying back and forth between the town council, the contractor and the GWR. After two further days had passed, something clearly had to be done. The contractor was promising to pay three days wages, out of the 12 owed. Reading Council opened its own bank account to hand each man a further six days pay, having been promised by the contractor that it would be swiftly reimbursed. The Mayor announced all this to the navvies in Forbury Square on Friday afternoon, a week after the trouble had started. After some shouting and a couple of speeches by leading navvies, the workmen agreed to return to their camp. That evening a long trail of hundreds of men wound out of Reading and back towards Sonning. The Guards left at the same time. Reading's most exciting week for generations was over.

A few days later the *Berkshire Chronicle* printed a leading article on the subject that concluded: 'The conduct pursued by the men under their privations has undoubtedly raised them in the estimation of those inhabitants of this town who had formerly but an indifferent opinion of the character of railroad labourers.'

The strike over, work continued. In April 1839 two men were killed in a landslide. The bodies were taken to Sonning church for burial, followed by a vast procession of navvies, marching in silence down from their workings on the hill. The vicar then treated the men to a long sermon on the sins of drunkenness, which seems a little harsh in the circumstances.

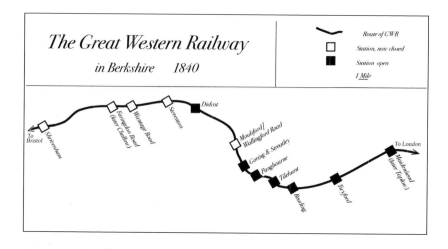

Although deaths in the cutting were fortunately rare – a third man died when trampled by a runaway horse and a fourth when a strong wind blew a shed roof on top of him – injuries were common. The GWR decided to make a donation of 100 guineas to the local Royal Berkshire Hospital, and undertook to pay a further 10 guineas each year.

Finally the line to Reading opened on 30 March 1840. Once over the Thames and through the cutting, construction of the railway speeded up. By December 1840 it was out of Berkshire and driving west. The line between London and Bristol was completed on 30 June 1841. Within a few years, numerous other rail lines were to be constructed both by the GWR and by other railway companies. One of the most important of these was to be the 1847 GWR line from Reading to Newbury and Hungerford.

By this time Brunel had hired as the GWR Superintendent of Locomotive Engines another innovative young engineer, the 21-year-old Daniel Gooch, later to be knighted, who proved to be an inspired choice both as an expert on locomotives and as a businessman. It was Gooch who, disappointed with the quality of locomotives made by contractors, persuaded the GWR to establish its own manufacturing centre at Swindon. In

PANGBOURNE STATION,

Pangbourne station as it stood in 1852. This layout of platforms facing each other across two rail lines, and the distinctive architecture of the main building is typical of GWR stations built by Brunel. (Taken from The Illustrated Guide to the Great Western Railway *by George Meason, 1852)*

September 1846 the first locomotive to be built by Gooch and his team at Swindon rolled out of the works. This was the 2-2-2 express passenger engine *Great Western*.

The 2-2-2 express locomotives came to be seen as distinctive of the GWR, as did the 2-2-2 Firefly class of less powerful locomotives for general work. A total of 62 Firefly engines were to be built in all. The most powerful of all the early engines was the 4-2-2 Iron Duke class, though only a handful were built.

It was appropriate that Gooch's first locomotive was an express, as the GWR was soon breaking all records for passenger speeds. The best known train was the *Flying Dutchman*, offering the fastest scheduled rail service in the world. It completed the 194 miles from Paddington to Exeter daily at an average speed of 53 mph, and reached Swindon at an incredible average of 59 mph. No other railway on earth could touch the broad gauge GWR for speed, comfort or reliability. By 1865 there were more than 800 miles of broad gauge running across the south and west of England and into southern Wales.

Similarly, Brunel's concept of a network of railways tying the country together and changing forever the social life of England became reality. Branch lines shot out from the GWR main line in

A stretch of broad gauge rail. Note how the rails run along the timber baulks, with spacing bars at infrequent intervals. (Courtesy of the Didcot Railway Centre)

all directions. Some were built by the GWR, others by independent rail companies.

By the 1870s people wanting to cover any distance at all did so by train and people were travelling a lot further and more often than they ever had before. Men no longer needed to reside within a few hundred yards of their place of work. They could live in one place and work in another – the commuter was born. Nor did people any longer mix only with people within their own immediate area. It has been estimated from parish records in one county that in 1800 men married women who lived, on average, three miles away. By 1900 men were marrying women who lived, on average, ten miles away.

Of course the huge growth in travel by rail, both passenger and freight, meant the collapse in prosperity of other modes of transport. Canals and river barges went first, as goods moving

An 0-6-2 engine that was a common sight on the Berkshire lines. (Courtesy of the Didcot Railway Centre)

between towns and cities switched to railways. The long-distance coaches followed them to oblivion very quickly, most routes ceasing to be run by the 1840s. Local coach routes prospered for a while. The most successful were those that linked towns to the nearest railway station. These were eventually undercut by the branch lines and by the 1880s there were effectively no scheduled horse coach lines left in England.

Despite the enormous success of the railways in general and the GWR in particular, the days of the grand vision that Brunel had in the 1830s and that Gooch helped bring to reality in the 1850s did not survive for long.

Already in the 1840s the successful and profitable GWR had begun buying up smaller railway companies that had lines in the west of the country. Almost without exception these lines operated on the standard gauge. At first it was more a nuisance than a problem to transfer goods and passengers from a broad

23

The Transfer Shed dating from the 1870s at the Didcot Railway Centre. Broad gauge goods trains stood in the right-hand bay and standard gauge trains in the left-hand bay while gangs of workers transferred goods between the two. (Courtesy of the Didcot Railway Centre)

gauge to a standard gauge train where such lines met, but by the 1860s the real profits were beginning to be made in long-distance through traffic. The various railway companies developed a fairly complex, but enormously successful, method of selling just one ticket to cover a journey across several lines, with the money being divided up among the companies concerned according to a set formula.

The GWR, with its broad gauge, was unable to take full advantage of the new system and began to suffer accordingly. At first it was decided to solve the problem by laying a third track on each line. This allowed broad gauge trains to run on the outer tracks, while standard gauge trains used one outer rail and the inner rail. As might have been expected, points and junctions

After it converted to standard gauge, the GWR could handle through freight trains from other networks. It was therefore able to carry a wide variety of trucks from far beyond its area of operations. (Courtesy of the Didcot Railway Centre)

were horrifically complex under this system. Costs began to spiral.

There might have been a solution to the problem, but by the late 1880s both Gooch and Brunel were dead. The board of the GWR decided to convert their entire network to standard gauge. Branch lines were converted first. The shorter ones were altered overnight, the longer ones after being closed for a day or two. By 1892 only the main line remained to be changed.

At midnight on Friday, 20 May the locomotives and rolling stock of the broad gauge lines began their last journey to Swindon for breaking up. By dawn all traffic was off the lines. As the sun came up, a massed workforce of 4,200 men set about their task. Following a detailed set of instructions that ran to over 70 pages, the foremen organised the work teams as the

A Collett 48xx class 0-4-2 tank engine, no 1466. This was built at Swindon in 1936 specifically to work the branch lines of the GWR. It saw service on several lines in Berkshire before being retired in the 1960s. (Courtesy of the Didcot Railway Centre)

A GWR Super Saloon carriage, introduced in 1931 to provide First Class accommodation on the trains that ran from London to Plymouth to link up with transatlantic liners. They were unique in having such large windows and sides that bowed out to provide a few extra inches of space inside for the passengers. (Courtesy of the Didcot Railway Centre)

The travelling post office. This specialised carriage contained teams of postmen who sorted out mail as the train raced towards its destination. The net was used to collect bags of mail suspended from special hooks at designated locations without the train slowing down. (Courtesy of the Didcot Railway Centre)

broad gauge track was torn up to be replaced by standard gauge line, with prefabricated junctions and points hauled into place from where they had been dropped off at trackside the previous day. The teams of men worked day and night that weekend and by 4 am on Monday morning the entire 177 miles of main line, plus many more miles of sidings, junctions and yards, had been converted. The work was finished several minutes early. At 4.04 am the night mail express pulled out of Plymouth heading for Penzance. It was the first train to run on the new lines.

That Monday morning the grand vision of Brunel died but much of his work can still be seen today. The Maidenhead bridge stands intact and unchanged by the passing years. Sonning Cutting is likewise still there, much as it was when the navvies left it. Some of his stations are in use, of which Cookham is perhaps the most charming, while Paddington in London is the most impressive. Most have been dramatically altered, however, as the passing years brought different demands that led to changes or rebuilding.

2
The Other Railways

The South Eastern Railway
The London and South Western Railway

An 0-4-2 tank engine prepares to haul a single carriage train out of Reading General in July 1957. Reading General was the name given to the old GWR Reading station during nationalisation.

The South Eastern Railway

Although most of Berkshire fell within the territory of the mighty Great Western Railway, the south-eastern corner of the county was contested between two other rail companies: The London and South Western Railway (LSWR) and the South Eastern Railway (SER).

First to arrive in the county was the SER. The rail links from

29

Ash Junction to Reading and from Reading to Guildford had been built by the smaller Reading, Guildford and Reigate Railway Company in 1849, but this company had been created with the close co-operation of the SER and was taken over by the larger company in 1852. After years of intense competition with the GWR, which ran trains from Paddington to its own Reading station, the SER came to an arrangement. Both companies agreed to charge identical fares for passengers, and the SER won some concessions on freight traffic. The agreement, and its successors, were to last some 85 years.

The first SER station at Reading was struck by lightning in 1859 and burned to the ground. The second station was opened the following year with a single platform, with two faces, and a large engine shed. In 1896 the engine shed was removed to make way for another two-faced platform. When nationalisation came after the Second World War it was decided to rename the SER Reading station as Reading Southern to avoid confusion with the GWR Reading station, which became Reading General. The SER goods yard, meanwhile, had expanded in 1899 and again in 1941 to cope with wartime traffic.

Soon after nationalisation a study was undertaken to see what savings could be made now that the various lines were no longer in the hands of competing private companies. The two stations at Reading, situated as they were so close to each other, were an obvious target for economies. It was the SER station that was earmarked for closure. A new platform, 4A, was built at Reading General to handle the trains that ran over the former SER lines. Reading Southern closed on 6 September 1965. Ten years later it was found that Reading General's platform 4A could not cope with the passenger trains, so a new platform 4B was built.

The goods yard of the old SER line continued in use for some years longer than the passenger station. But freight traffic was also declining. In September 1970 most of the yard was closed down, with only a siding dedicated to the huge Huntley and Palmer's biscuit factory being kept in operation. In April 1979 that, too, closed.

Today nothing is left of the old SER station at Reading. All the land has been sold off for office and commercial developments.

Bracknell station on the LSWR line from Wokingham to Staines, as it appeared in the 1890s. The station was opened in 1856 and had been little altered by the time this photo was taken.

An undated view of Bracknell station, taken from the opposite end of the platform, looking towards Reading. The station was almost completely swept away when the area was redeveloped in 1976. The buildings are now much smaller and nondescript, most of the land having been sold off for redevelopment as offices. Only the footbridge remains in situ.

The London and South Western Railway

What was to become a LSWR line ran from Wokingham to Staines by way of Ascot and opened on 9 July 1856. The line was built by the Staines, Wokingham and Woking Junction Railway Company, but the trains were from the start operated by the LSWR. In 1878 the LSWR bought out the SWWJR.

Apart from Ascot West station (a non-passenger stop) on the LSWR line and Reading Southern, all the stations on the SER and LSWR lines in Berkshire remain open. Although freight has collapsed, the commuter traffic has increased enormously and now supplies nearly all of the thousands of people who use these lines daily.

3
The Horse Train To Lambourn

Lambourn Valley Railway

Lambourn station in the early 1950s, looking towards Newbury. The water tower and main passenger platform can be seen clearly. None of this now remains.

The Lambourn Valley is a charming rural corner of Berkshire that has escaped the rush and bustle afflicting so much of the Royal County. The waters of the Lambourn run clear and cool, rising from the chalk downs that surround the valley. They burble down through green fields, forming extensive ponds and winding through meadows and flourishing woodlands.

No wonder the Lambourn line was regarded as one of the most scenic on the Great Western Railway network throughout its life.

But it was not the scenery that brought the railway to the valley so much as hard economic facts. In the 1870s the smooth grassy hills above Lambourn were home to dozens of the most successful racehorse training stables in England – as they remain today. But the stable managers had a problem. When a race meeting was due they had to ride their horses down to Newbury to be loaded onto trains for transportation to the racecourses. This involved tiring the horses, so they had to be rested for a day or two before they could be raced. Clearly there was a demand for a rail line to carry horses from Lambourn to the main Great Western Railway line at Newbury.

But the horses would need moving only prior to race days, and the railway would need traffic every day if it was to be economic. It was this that led to the cancellation of the first attempt to lay tracks up the valley when in 1873 the Didcot, Newbury and Southampton Junction Railway announced plans to run a horse-drawn tramway to Lambourn. The first rails were spiked by the Mayor of Newbury and the Countess of Craven under the guidance of E.E Allen, Chief Engineer, but the construction work only got as far as Donnington Square before the directors of the company stepped in to stop building. They had done the sums and believed the line would fail to make a profit.

All was not lost, however, and in 1881 the Independent Lambourn Valley Railway Company Ltd (ILVR) was founded under the chairmanship of Colonel Archer-Houblon. As the owner of Welford Park, the Colonel had a vested interest in seeing a railway built up the valley and he recruited a number of local businessmen and worthies to his cause. He, too, had done his financial sums and believed that the railway could run at a profit. In addition to the racehorses and passengers, Archer-Houblon looked to coal to pay his way.

Before the widespread use of electricity or gas in houses, it was coal that supplied the fuel for domestic heating and cooking. Fires were lit in rooms, or else they became very cold

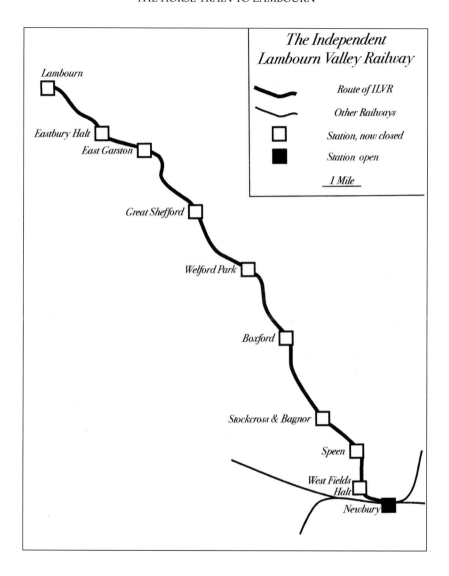

in winter. And every house or cottage had a range in the kitchen on which to cook food or heat water for baths. All this used up vast amounts of coal, which was bulky and heavy to transport.

Colonel Archer-Houblon estimated that he could transport coal from Newbury depot to Lambourn at a tenth of the cost charged by the horse and cart contractors. He could halve the price to the householders of the Lambourn Valley and still turn a handsome profit.

In 1888 J.E. Billups of Tredegarville, Cardiff, was awarded the contract for building the railway and on 18 June work began. The Great Western Railway had agreed to allow the Lambourn Valley line to install a bay platform, no 3, at Newbury station and to run their tracks alongside those of the main London–West of England line for half a mile to get their line out of what was then the built-up area of Newbury.

The route then turned north-west, crossing the canal and the Kennet river, then cutting through a hill to reach Speen. It was this section that would prove to be the most troublesome to build and maintain.

Beyond Speen the route ran alongside the river to Boxford, with an intermediate station – Stockcross & Bagnor. Reaching Boxford necessitated building a small embankment, after which the track crossed level ground to reach Welford Park.

As the home of the company's chairman and chief promoter, Welford Park was inevitably given the finest station on the route. It had separate up and down platforms, a waiting room and a siding – such were the benefits of being the top executive. Beyond Welford Park, the track ran fairly straight to Great Shefford, where a goods yard was erected. This included a scissors crossover giving access to a twin-track siding on which was a cattle-loading dock.

The line then ran across a gentle gradient to East Garston, from here the steepest gradient of the entire line, about 1:60, went up to Eastbury. A much gentler 1:100 gradient then continued to Lambourn itself. Although the GWR had allocated space for a bay platform at Newbury, possibilities there were restricted, so it was at Lambourn that the main depot was constructed. Initially this consisted of a two-platform station with signal box, loading docks for general goods and specialised ones for racehorses, and offices for the railway staff. There was also a train shed, in which the rolling stock was stored when not

Great Sheffort Station. L. V. Ry.

A pannier tank engine waits patiently at Great Shefford on its way to Lambourn in 1912. (Courtesy of Lens of Sutton)

in use. For a 12 mile line, most of which was single track, the station at Lambourn was both extensive and impressive.

In 1890 the construction of the line was nearing completion when disaster struck. The cutting beside Bath Road, just outside Newbury, collapsed. Billups blamed the railway for choosing a route that cut through unstable substrata, while the railway blamed Billups for not constructing the cutting banks correctly. The arguments and disputes dragged on for a year and ended up in the courts. The judge found in favour of the railway, forcing Billups to pay a substantial sum for the failed works and to return much of their fees.

The ILVR then called in S. Pearson and Son, a British company that had moved to the U.S.A. and was then involved with the construction of railroads in North and Central America. Pearson and Son finished the work and just after Christmas 1897 the first locomotive ran along the newly completed line. This was an 0-6-0 ST locomotive named *Ernest*, which bore the number 594 from the Hunslet Engine Company of Leeds. *Ernest* was the works locomotive of Pearson's, carrying building materials and workmen to complete the various stations and loading docks along the route. In April 1898 the building work was finally done, *Ernest* left to work on newer lines elsewhere and the Lambourn Valley had its new railway line.

It did not, however, have either locomotives or rolling stock. The ILVR seems to have been caught rather by surprise at the speed with which Pearson's completed the work. But if the new railway was to make money, it had to have trains. Colonel Archer-Houblon turned first to the GWR. The larger concern readily agreed to rent two locomotives to the ILVR, but did not have any spare rolling stock.

Archer-Houblon could not raise any new money from his backers, so he put his hand into his own pocket to buy the necessary carriages and wagons. He signed a hire-purchase agreement with the ILVR under which the stock remained the Colonel's property until such time as the company had paid off their cost. The stock purchased by Archer-Houblon came in the shape of 12 second-hand goods wagons bought from the Metropolitan Railway Carriage and Wagon Co for £189 and six second-hand wagons purchased from the GWR for £91 10s. The Colonel opted to splash out on a bit more luxury for the passengers, acquiring brand new carriages that contained both 1st Class and 2nd Class seating. Each coach was 26 feet 6 inches in length with an open platform at each end and a central gangway. The 1st Class seats were beautifully upholstered, but 2nd Class passengers had to make do with wooden benches. The coaches could seat 32 people each and had their own vacuum brakes for safety. They cost the Colonel the grand sum of £1,300. To leave no doubt in anyone's mind, Archer-Houblon had a brass plate affixed to each coach reading 'This coach is the property of Colonel Archer-Houblon of Welford Park, Newbury'.

Thus equipped, the ILVR went into operation.

On 31 March 1898 Colonel Yorke of the Board of Trade inspected the new railway. He gave the track, facilities and rolling stock a clean bill of health, but imposed a speed limit of 25 mph and a maximum axle loading of 8 tons.

The opening ceremony took place on Saturday, 2 April with the inaugural train pulling into platform 3 at Newbury at 10.30 am. The locomotive, no 1384, was decorated with bunting, flags and a portrait of Queen Victoria, which was fixed between the front buffers. Colonel Archer-Houblon made a short speech to the assembled guests, dignitaries and prospective passengers before, at 11 am, the guard called 'Take your seats please'. Most of the guests had seating in the carriages, but the local Member of Parliament, Mr W.G. Mount, was allowed on to the footplate.

Under the guidance of the driver, Mr Mount operated the controls to get the train under way. Amid much hissing and puffing, the first train to run on the ILVR pulled out of Newbury. Exactly 37 minutes later it arrived at Lambourn to be welcomed by a brass band, peals from the parish church bells and a sizeable crowd. The train ran back and forth three times that first day, then regular scheduled services began on the following Monday. Over 900 people travelled on the railway in its first week, and a race meeting meant that dozens of horses were transported as well. And the coal trade was also quick off the marks. All seemed set fair for the profitability of the new railway.

Behind the scenes, however, there were problems. The two engines rented from GWR were proving to be expensive and the search was on for replacements. The Chief Engineer, Mr J. McIntyre, eventually found two engines of which he approved, and at a price of which Colonel Archer-Houblon approved. The two 0-6-0 side tank locomotives were bought from Chapman and Furneaux of Gateshead for £1,330 each. They arrived in October 1898 in a smart dark blue livery, with black linings edged in white.

The new trains were named *Aelfred* and *Ealhswith*, after King Alfred the Great and his wife. Alfred, local tradition had it, had inflicted a defeat on the Vikings on a hill just outside Lambourn in the year AD 871. The two locomotives performed well, keeping the trains running regularly – and profitably. The company made an operating profit of about £1,000 in its first 12 months, though after moneys owed to the Colonel were taken into account there was a small loss.

The 0-6-0 tank locomotive Ealhswith pulls into Lambourn c.1902, hauling its usual three carriages. The building behind the train is probably the engine shed.

At the other end of its run, the Ealhswith stands at Newbury, facing towards Lambourn. In the foreground is the loop track that enabled the tank engines to change ends on the train before returning down the line.

By Christmas 1902 it was obvious that the locomotives were going to need some maintenance that would take them out of use for some time. The company therefore bought a third 0-6-0 locomotive, this time from the Hunslet Engine Company. It was named *Eadweade*, after the son of Alfred the Great and Queen Ealhswith who inherited the throne after his father's death and inflicted further defeats on the Vikings.

In September 1903 the directors of the ILVR were surprised to receive a formal offer from the GWR to buy the railway outright for the sum of £45,000. The offer was turned down as the railway was operating at a profit, though only just, and the directors were confident that it had a healthy future ahead of it. In January 1904 GWR tried again with an offer of £50,000 and again were turned down.

Despite the rebuffs, the GWR and ILVR remained on good terms and continued to run their services in co-operation with

A GWR steam railmotor, a revolutionary vehicle that combined a steam locomotive and passenger seating in one vehicle. The GWR built 99 of these and, although they were not a success on the Lambourn branch due to the chalky nature of the local water, they did sterling service elsewhere on the network.

each other. In May 1904, for instance, the ILVR sold their locomotives and instead began renting railmotors from the GWR. The change allowed Colonel Archer-Houblon to be at last fully repaid for his initial outlay. This seems to have been the catalyst for a major shake-up. In January 1905 the ILVR approved an offer from the GWR to purchase the branch line in its entirety for £50,000. After details of the deal had been cleared up, it was finalised at simultaneous meetings of both boards of directors at Paddington on 19 July 1905.

The new owners at once set about a major programme of changes and improvements. The GWR had a fine reputation for top quality engineering and careful attention to passenger comfort and freight safety. The engineers of the GWR had already decided that the track, buildings and engineering of the ILVR did not come up to their exacting standards. They went to work and, with their customary skill and regard for profits, kept the trains running throughout the work.

The first problem to be addressed was that the platforms were not high enough to allow passengers to step straight onto carriages. The ILVR had expected passengers to climb up a couple of steps, but the GWR would not ask this of its passengers, so every platform at every station had to be altered. The main station at Lambourn was completely rebuilt with modern brick-built facilities and a new halt was installed at 'Newbury West Fields'. All stations received new lamp-posts, name-boards and benches, while new passing loops were installed at Welford Park, Great Shefford, East Garston and Boxford. Over the next five years the entire track was re-laid. In all, the GWR spent about £75,000 on its improvements.

In 1912 the GWR increased the number of trains, including a new Sunday service consisting of two passenger runs each way. Sadly, this improved service did not last long. In October 1914 the GWR introduced revised timetables to take account of the needs of the Great War on which the country had now embarked. The Lambourn line saw services cut back considerably and the Sunday service was axed.

When peace came, the Lambourn line saw increased service with five passenger runs being made each weekday. In 1924 a

An 0-6-0 PT at Newbury station in 1964. This engine is hauling two goods wagons, indicating that it has come along a branch line, most likely the Lambourn Valley. (Courtesy of D. E. Canning)

Sunday milk train was introduced, linking to a similar train running from Didcot to Southampton. The branch line was now at its most profitable. The income was double that of 1913 and would soon increase again. The racehorse business was booming and up to 35 horseboxes travelled from Lambourn to Newbury, and thence to distant racecourses, the day before important race meets. In 1932 a new late-evening Saturday service was introduced and proved to be hugely popular with residents of the Lambourn Valley returning home after an evening out in Newbury.

Unfortunately, though, a decline in demand was on its way. The underlying problem was the loss of the trade that Colonel Archer-Houblon had identified as the steady income generator. Domestic coal was not being used in such huge quantities as before. Both electricity and gas were gradually being introduced to the villages around Lambourn, as elsewhere. People found that gas cookers, gas heaters and electric lights were far more

43

The Lambourn train waits in its bay, ready to leave Newbury. In 1929 the GWR bought three 2-4-0 tender engines from the Midland and South Western Junction Railway for use on its longer branch lines. One of these engines is shown here together with an odd mix of near obsolete passenger coaches.

clean, safe and convenient than coal. Slowly the dirty, heavy coal was ousted from houses, and the demand for it fell accordingly.

By 1936 the line was making a small loss. The GWR took prompt action. West Fields, Stockcross and Eastbury were left unmanned, and the train guard was given the task of selling and checking tickets. In 1937 a diesel railcar was introduced. Able to pull a tail load of 60 tons, the railcar could cope with the trains on the Lambourn line and was considerably cheaper to run than the old steam engines. In 1938 the line made a small profit again.

In 1938 a threat to the passenger business arrived in the shape of a bus operated by the Thames Valley Traction Company. The bus was cheaper than the railway, but ran only on the busiest days: Thursday and Saturday. It creamed off the passengers on those days, leaving the railway to deal with passengers for the rest of the week.

A streamlined GWR diesel railcar of the type that ran on the Lambourn branch towards the end of the life of that line. (Courtesy of Mr W.P. Ruane)

The Second World War, of course, changed everything. In the short term the war was good for the Lambourn line. Several military camps were set up in the valley, generating both passengers and goods for the railway. As a branch line, the Lambourn Valley suffered neither chronic over use nor the attentions of the Luftwaffe and ended the war in a good condition, from the engineering point of view.

From a business viewpoint, however, the Lambourn line was severely affected. What demand had remained for coal collapsed soon after the war, while the racehorse business was in a severe depression. And refrigerated trucks, developed to help shift war supplies, now took the milk traffic off the branch line.

On 1 January 1948 British Railways took over a branch line that was losing money quickly. The new management axed the Sunday goods train and reduced Boxford to the status of an unmanned halt. In 1956 the diesel railcar was removed for service elsewhere and replaced by antiquated steam engines not

A view of Lambourn station taken in the 1950s. (Courtesy of D. E. Canning)

required on more important routes. Passenger numbers continued to fall. In 1957 West Fields Halt was closed and the small waiting room demolished.

Still passenger numbers fell as buses and private motor cars became more numerous and popular. In June 1959 BR announced that the Lambourn line had become economically unviable. It was to close to passengers in January 1960.

The last day of passenger services to Lambourn proved to be almost as celebratory as the first day. Large numbers of passengers turned out and the trains were packed as they ran in both directions. At 5.20 pm the last train, of six coaches, pulled out of Lambourn for Newbury. The line was closed.

In 1962, by which time it was clear the rail service would not be reintroduced, the line was lifted beyond Welford Park and sold for scrap.

But all was not yet lost. In 1952 a short spur had been built from Welford Park to the American air base at Welford. This

A chilly scene taken amid the snow of 14 February 1962 as a train pulls into Stockcross station on the Lambourn Valley Line. This was a notoriously cold winter when the snow fell in late December, but did not melt until March. (Courtesy of D. E. Canning)

generated large quantities of goods traffic as supplies, equipment and weaponry were moved to and from the base by rail. This service was profitable for BR, so the line to Welford Park, and the spur beyond, remained in place and in operation. For a while general goods trains ran to Welford Park, but by 1966 this too was losing money and the service closed.

In 1973, however, the US military decided to shift all transport from rail to road. The military supply trains stopped running and the remaining track and buildings stood empty and disused. In 1976 BR engaged Thomas Ward & Co of Sheffield to remove and sell anything that could be scrapped, and to demolish what was left. By the end of 1977 the work was complete.

The Lambourn Valley Railway was gone.

But it was not forgotten. Some of the equipment and the waiting room from Stockcross were taken to Didcot Rail Centre,

A group of enthusiasts watch the last day special train running along the Lambourn Valley line at Speen Crossing on 3 November 1973. (Courtesy of D. E. Canning)

Remnants of Stockcross & Bagnor station, as rebuilt at the Didcot Railway Centre. The unusual pagoda-style waiting room was a standard feature of all stations on the Lambourn line. (Courtesy of the Didcot Railway Centre)

where they can be visited today. And, of course, the route of the railway remained although the fact that little in the way of heavy engineering had been required means that the exact route can be difficult to trace on the ground.

The section of the line closest to Newbury has been obliterated by modern building and road construction. While traces of the old route can be picked out here and there, it does not really become clear and continuous until close to Boxford. A clearly visible embankment runs south of the village, while an equally obvious cutting runs to the north. The former station of Welford Park now stands adjacent to, and forms part of, the car park used by visitors to Welford Park itself. The platforms can be made out with ease, as can the railbed and, with a bit more imagination, the goods loading bay. All the buildings have, however, long

The remains of Welford Park station. The buildings have been demolished, but the platforms were simply left to rot. This photo shows the main trackbed running between the two platforms, looking towards Newbury.

The view looking towards Lambourn from the ruins of Welford Park station. In the foreground is the car park for Welford Park, occupying the flat ground once covered by the trackbed and freight yard. The shadows show where the old line entered a short cutting.

The Welford Park ticket office survived the demolition of the station in the 1970s and was taken to Didcot for preservation. It is now in use as a ticket office on the branch line. (Courtesy of the Didcot Railway Centre)

The lifting of the Lambourn Valley bay at Newbury in 1968. The tracks here had been left in place after the line closed, but by 1968 were no longer needed. (Courtesy D. E. Canning)

gone. Welford Park is famous for its snowdrops, and is open during the flowering season, at which time the old station site can be viewed. Opening times are available on the website www.welfordpark.co.uk.

Beyond Welford, the old route runs through a short cutting before running across open land, where it is effectively invisible. At Lambourn itself the station buildings were all demolished and were replaced by an industrial estate. This has in turn largely gone, to be replaced by a housing estate. The only sign of the vanished railway is found in the name of the estate: Old Station Yard.

51

4
The Didcot, Newbury And Southampton Railway

A pair of King class locomotives wait at Newbury racecourse beneath the traditional signals in 1962. (Courtesy of D. E. Canning)

The longest, busiest and most scenic of all the lost railways of Berkshire was very nearly never built at all. Only the prompt intervention of a war hero and local celebrity saved the project from being abandoned before it had really begun.

The main impetus behind the railway came from the city of Southampton. By 1846 the docks at Southampton were losing out to rivals along the south coast. The town council believed that the lack of a direct rail route inland, running north to the industrial heartlands, was the chief cause of a lack of business. The only rail line ran from Southampton to London, part of the network of the London and South Western Railway (LSWR). This route provided only a very circuitous route to the Midlands and was deemed to be ineffective by the authorities in Southampton. Several routes running north from Southampton became the subject of interest from surveyors working for speculative rail entrepreneurs, though no project actually came to fruition.

One entrepreneur went by the name of John Bethell, a solicitor who acted on behalf of the rather grandly named Oxford, Southampton, Gosport and Portsmouth Railway Company Ltd. Despite its title, the railway was not intended actually to reach any of the places named. Instead it was to consist of a line running from the GWR station of Didcot to the LSWR station at Micheldever. The line would cut off the lengthy roundabout route that was then the only way to travel by rail between these two stations. In effect it would have provided a much shorter route between Oxford and the southern towns that then existed. In the event the line failed to gain Parliamentary approval, and was dropped. But it was not forgotten.

In 1873 a new company was founded, the Didcot, Newbury and Southampton Junction Railway. This new company was the brainchild of a London lawyer named William Tatham. He had simply dusted down the old route envisaged by Bethell, but he added an important new financial consideration. The vast majority of ocean trade was by this date being carried in steam ships, whereas in the 1840s it had gone by sail. Southampton was now in desperate need of a direct rail route to the coalfields so that the vast quantities of bulky, heavy coal needed to re-supply merchant ships could be transported cheaply and reliably. Again, the existing circuitous LSWR route was proving to be unsatisfactory.

Armed with his new business plan for the old route, Tatham signed up three City gentlemen as directors and put a Bill before Parliament. The Bill duly became the Didcot, Newbury and Southampton Junction Railway Act on 5 August 1873. Tatham deposited the £30,000 – then a colossal sum – required by Parliament as a guarantee of his good faith and set about the lengthy business of raising capital for his scheme. He did not do very well. In 1876 a meeting of the Board of Directors took place at which two of the three directors resigned. The only reason the third did not resign was that he did not bother turning up.

Tatham was left with an empty shell of a company, no backers and no directors. In 1879 he asked Parliament to return his deposit. This involved the repealing of the Didcot, Newbury and Southampton Junction Railway Act and the abandonment of the

A general view of Didcot taken in about 1960 showing both up and down platforms. The City of Truro locomotive can be seen waiting in the bay platform. It will soon be heading for Newbury. (Courtesy of Lens of Sutton)

entire scheme. The repeal was hurried through the House of Commons without any opposition and passed two of its three readings in the House of Lords just as quickly.

At which point the imposing figure of Sir Robert Loyd-Lindsay VC entered the story. Loyd-Lindsay had been born just plain Robert Lindsay in Scotland in 1832, and he followed his father into the army at the age of 18. On 20 September 1854 the then Captain Lindsay found himself in command of a company of the Scots Fusilier Guards at the Battle of the Alma, in the Crimean War. Lindsay and his men had advanced over the river when the regiment was overwhelmed by a counterattack by Russian infantry. Lindsay grabbed the Queen's Colours, rallied a small group of men and fought his way to safety with the precious colours still intact. As a result he received the very first Victoria Cross ever to be awarded.

Lindsay returned to Britain and on 26 June 1857 had the medal pinned on his chest by Queen Victoria herself. The dashing young hero became the most celebrated figure in London society. He met and married Harriet, the only daughter and sole heir to the astonishingly wealthy Lord Overstone. Lindsay adopted his wife's surname of Loyd in addition to his own and in due course the couple inherited Lord Overstone's 20,000 acre estate – the largest in Berkshire. He also got himself elected to be Member of Parliament for Berkshire and took a keen interest in the Didcot, Newbury and Southampton Junction Railway Act, as the proposed route ran adjacent to his lands.

Loyd-Lindsay had been looking forward to making use of the new railway and was deeply disappointed to learn that it faced extinction. He was joined in his disappointment by his fellow parliamentarian, Henry, 4th Earl of Carnarvon, who also owned extensive lands close to the proposed route. Carnarvon was not simply a wealthy landowner, but also a member of the government. His influence, and the cash the two men could deposit, secured the rapid transfer of the Didcot, Newbury and Southampton Railway Co Ltd (DN&SR), as it became, into their own hands.

On 26 August 1879 Lady Carnarvon performed the ceremonial turning of the first sod in the construction of the new railway. The ceremony took place in a field next to London Road at Didcot. It was an inauspicious start as torrential rain fell all day and everyone involved was soaked to the skin. Nevertheless work was under way. Loyd-Lindsay became Chairman of the Board and recruited as his fellow directors W.G. Mount, later MP for Newbury, and John Walter, the then owner of *The Times* newspaper. The highly experienced John Fowler was hired as Engineer while Falkiner and Tancred were engaged as the contractors for construction.

With such impressive backers, the DN&SR had little trouble raising money. A total of £300,000 was accumulated by selling shares and another £98,800 by the sale of a debenture stock paying 5%. Thus equipped with funds, the DN&SR began construction work. The first section to be built was the 17 miles between Didcot and Newbury, the part of the line that lay in Berkshire. Although only a single track was laid down, the roadway, bridges and other features were all built to allow for a double track as it was confidently expected that the railway would one day be so busy as to justify the improvement.

John Fowler recommended that the railway should follow a slightly different route to that envisaged by Bethell, so fresh Parliamentary approval was needed. This was gained in July 1880, after which construction work was rapid. The new route was needed partly due to a more detailed survey that had been undertaken, but perhaps just as importantly due to the need to provide a station close to Loyd-Lindsay's estates.

This station, Churn, was very much a personal matter. Trains stopped here only when requested to do so by Loyd-Lindsay or his guests. None of the schedules mentioned the stop at all. It stood at the very crest of the route, 379 feet above sea level on the wide, open grassy downs. Close by, Loyd-Lindsay constructed a rifle range, which generated a fair amount of traffic at times.

From Didcot the railway swung south to climb gently for a mile or so as it left the town and passed East Hagbourne. The line then began a lengthy climb, at a gradient, of 1:106 along an embankment that in places was 33 feet high to the station at Upton, where the gradient was reduced to 1:530 in the station and for a short distance either side. The line then resumed its

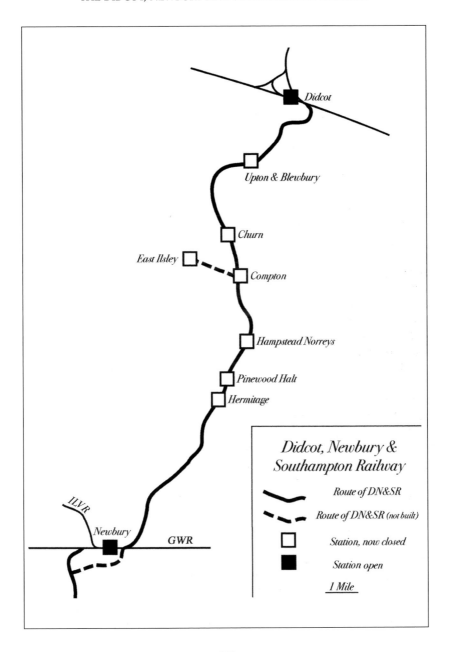

climb at 1:106 as it plunged into a massive cutting that swept in a great curve around the hill south of Upton Lodge.

In places the Upton Cutting was 50 feet deep, and along much of its length was around 40 feet deep. In all some 400,000 cubic feet of chalk had to be excavated to make this cutting. It was an awesome task, but the Scottish contractors, Falkiner and Tancred, were equal to the work. They brought in what they termed a 'steam navvy' to carry out the work. This was a steam-powered digging machine that hacked its way through the chalk hills much more quickly than could the traditional teams of navvies – men armed with picks and shovels. The machine became something of a novelty while it was at work, attracting sightseers from the nearby towns and villages.

The line emerged from the cutting after almost two miles to proceed onto the open downs at Churn station. Beyond Churn, the line began a gentle descent over the Blewbury Downs at gradients varying between 1:264 and 1:1375. After two miles the line reached the station of Compton.

This station was conveniently located between the church and the pub that served the village. It was also the largest access point to the DN&SR between Didcot and Newbury. There was not only a loop, but also sidings and an engine shed. This was the main station for what was to become an important business on this northern section of the line: horseboxes. The downs made ideal country for the keeping and training of racehorses. Indeed, the area around Churn is still criss-crossed by extensive gallops and practice racecourses. Racehorses were brought down to Compton to be loaded into horseboxes for transportation to racecourses around the country.

At Compton the line picked up the headwaters of the River Pang, and followed the banks of the babbling chalk stream down along a gradient of some 1:178 to the village of Hampstead Norreys, where another station was constructed. There the line left the stream to begin a two mile climb at 1:106 to cross the top of the Newbury Downs just north of the village of Hermitage. Some years later, a small halt, named Pinewood, would be installed on the crest of the downs. The line levelled out to 1:330 for a short distance here where a station was built. The presence

Upton and Blewbury station in 1931. This was the first on the DN&SR south of Didcot. Most of the stations were built to a similar design, though as here a variety of additional storage sheds and lock-ups were added over the years.

Upton and Blewbury today, seen from the opposite side. The bridge visible in the earlier photo has been removed and the road now merely goes over a short rise, from which this picture was taken. The platform now forms a patio, while the tracks have been lifted and the soil profile smoothed over. A new house has been built on the site of the additional sheds and storage visible in the older photo. These days the station is a private house.

59

A diesel unit trundles past Compton Crossing on the Didcot-Newbury-Southampton line in 1963. (Courtesy of D. E. Canning)

of the Brains Brickworks at Hermitage provided so much goods traffic that special sidings were built from the station to the works.

From Hermitage, the line then began a four mile descent, mostly at 1:106 but in places 1:244, to reach the valley of the Kennet. The line joined the GWR main line just east of Newbury.

The line was therefore of a much gentler gradient throughout than was normal for branch lines over hilly country. The reason was that the company expected to be hauling heavy goods trains carrying coal and industrial goods to and from the port of Southampton. Steep gradients and sudden changes of slope therefore had to be avoided.

The route approved in 1880 called for the line to cross the GWR, loop around the south of Newbury and then continue south. In the event this short stretch was never built and the DN&SR trains ran over the GWR lines through Newbury and used the town's GWR station. The 1880 Act had likewise authorised a spur branch leaving Compton to run west over the downs to East Ilsley. It was proposed that this spur should be built later when traffic demanded it, but in the event it did not materialise.

Throughout its length the DN&SR adopted a unique design that is generally recognised as being one of the most charming and attractive of all the branch lines that ran off the GWR. The bricks used were of a mellow shade of red, and the majority of bridges were of brick arch design rather than steel girder. The station buildings themselves had high-arched dormer windows projecting from the roofline while the gable ends were highly decorated with fretwork. The layout of the stations was always neat and tidy, with none of the apparently haphazard jumble of sidings, loops and passenger facilities that were a feature of many small railways.

South of Newbury the DN&SR very quickly left Berkshire. Although the southern section of the route lies outside the scope

A pair of Castle class locomotives at Newbury racecourse station in 1962. (Courtesy of D. E. Canning)

of this book, it is important as its tortuous progress into reality had a serious effect on the levels of through traffic running over the Berkshire section. As originally envisaged, the railway was to run from Southampton to Didcot. The earlier plans drawn up by Bethell had involved trains running over LSWR tracks from Micheldever to Southampton. By 1880 the LSWR was no longer willing to go along with such an arrangement as the tracks were full to capacity with their own trains. The DN&SR therefore surveyed a route that would take their line by way of Whitchurch, Winchester and Chilworth to the docks at Southampton.

This move needed a new Act of Parliament and the DN&SR at once ran into trouble. The LSWR was a large and important company with plenty of influence in Parliament. They opposed the new line as it would take traffic off their route and so cost them money. The LSWR put forward a substitute scheme that would see a line built from the DN&SR at Whitchurch to the LSWR at Fullerton. Trains on the DN&SR would then use LSWR rails from Fullerton to Southampton. The DN&SR refused to be fobbed off with rights to run trains over a slow branch line.

The situation was complicated by the involvement of the GWR. For many years the two mighty rail companies, the LSWR and the GWR, had operated a gentleman's agreement regarding smaller companies such as the DN&SR. They had carved up western England between themselves into spheres of influence. The two companies agreed neither to support new lines nor to take over struggling small lines in each other's territory.

The LSWR had recently broken the agreement by purchasing the Somerset and Dorset Railway, which lay within the GWR area. Furthermore the LSWR was showing signs of wanting to repeat the trick in Devon. The GWR therefore stepped in to support the DN&SR in their bid to get their own lines down to the docks in Southampton.

The three-way intrigues, compromises and suggested deals dragged on for years. Eventually, the DN&SR was built only as far as Winchester. There, coaches and trucks had to be uncoupled and shunted to the LSWR tracks, where LSWR engines took them on to Southampton. The arrangement was

A diesel train pulls out of Newbury heading west in 1963. (Courtesy of D. E. Canning)

not ideal and suited nobody. The main importance of the decision for the stretch of line in Berkshire was that through freight traffic was always much lighter than had been expected, making the line much less profitable than had been hoped.

While the disputes over the southern route dragged on, the northern section of the DN&SR was completed. On 12 April 1882 the formal opening of the line took place. The GWR provided 30 special saloon cars, divided into two trains, to run from Newbury to Didcot. The opening ceremony was performed by Lady Loyd-Lindsay, soon to become Lady Wantage when Sir Robert was raised to the peerage. She cut a ribbon and made a short speech on a platform erected on the London Road bridge, just outside Newbury. A noisy salute of anvils followed, as gunpowder charges were set off between pairs of anvils. The two special trains then set off, waved on their way by a crowd of thousands that had gathered at Newbury station. The trains were met at Didcot by more cheering crowds. The events were

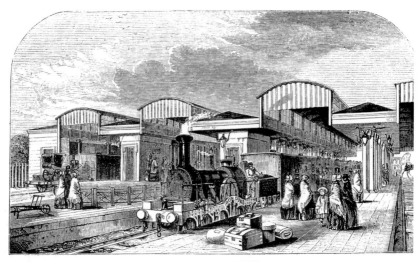

DIDCOT STATION

When Didcot station was built by Brunel it was designed to be one of the main stations on the GWR. As such it was ideally suited to host the northern end of the DN&SR. (Taken from The Illustrated Guide to the Great Western Railway *by George Meason, 1852)*

captured by an artist from *The London Graphic*, which published several pages of copy and illustrations to celebrate the opening of the new railway.

The full public service between Newbury and Didcot opened the following day. There were to be five passenger trains each way on weekdays only, with no passenger service at the weekends. Sir Robert and Lord Carnarvon were frank about their lack of experience of actually running a railway. They therefore opted to contract in services, and the GWR provided engines, rolling stock and train crew for the DN&SR in return for 60%, later reduced to 51.5%, of the fares and freight charges.

The GWR usually provided tank engines for use on the Newbury–Didcot section of the DN&SR. At first this was because of the lack of a turntable, which was planned for further south. When the southern section of the line was completed,

A 2-6-2 tank engine of the type that was widely used for branch line work on the Western Region. (Courtesy of D. E. Canning)

with its turntable, tender engines could and did run from Newbury to Didcot. The tanks remained more usual, however, with engines of the 2-4-0 Metropolitan class or 2-6-2 engines of the 6100 class being common. Passenger coaches were almost always older rolling stock that the GWR did not want to use on its own lines and routes.

In 1883 Loyd-Lindsay suffered a sudden bout of serious ill health. His doctor ordered complete rest and a prolonged holiday in sunnier climes. Carnarvon turned to James Forbes, who was already Chairman of the London, Chatham and Dover Railway, to take over. It was Forbes who abandoned the idea of pushing the DN&SR line to Southampton docks, opting to link with the LSWR at Winchester instead. And it was Forbes who oversaw the opening of the line along its entire length in 1891.

In 1894 there was a form of coup within the management of

A 2-6-2 steams gently on its way out of Newbury along the Didcot-Newbury-Southampton branch line that ran alongside the mainline for half a mile, as here at Gyers Lock Bridge, before branching off south. (Courtesy of D. E. Canning)

the DN&SR. The Berkshire landowners who had been the prime movers in the construction and initial funding of the line were replaced by businessmen from Southampton. Prominent among these were G.T. Harper, a shipbroker, Beresford Turner, Chairman of the Southampton Harbour Board, J.E. LeFeuvre of the Southampton Chamber of Commerce and Colonel E. Bance, one-time Mayor of Southampton. Forbes was quickly ousted as Chairman, his place being taken by G.T. Harper.

One of the first actions of the new board was to hire a Traffic Agent in the form of W.H.H.M. Gipps and to give him the task of generating freight traffic for the line. Gipps was a highly experienced and well respected figure in railway circles. The DN&SR could not afford his services, so they decided to share him with the Lambourn Valley Railway, where he worked as General Manager.

This through ticket is issued subject to the conditions and reg ations referred to in the Time Tables Bills and Notices of the respective Companies & Persons on whose Railways Coaches or Steamboats it is available and the holder by accepting it agrees that such Companies & Persons are not to be liable for any damage injury delay or detention caused or arising off their respective Railways Coaches or Steamboats. The contract and liability of each Company & Person are limited to their and his Railways Coaches and Steamboats.

Sold in September 1897, this ticket from Newbury to Southampton specifies that the traveller had to use the DN&SR lines down to Winchester and then the LSWR to Southampton. The ticket was sold by the GWR, which then allocated funds to the DN&SR and LSWR according to an agreed formula.

Gipps and his team of three worked wonders. Within ten years they had more than doubled the freight traffic to a respectable £19 10s 8d per mile per week. One of the most serious handicaps Gipps faced was the refusal of the LSWR and GWR to book cheaper through rates for goods wagons running from Southampton, up the DN&SR and on from Didcot. Wagons had to be booked first from Southampton to Winchester, then from Winchester to Didcot and finally from Didcot to their final destination. There was always the risk of delay at each handover. For most freight this was a serious inconvenience but for perishable foodstuffs it could be ruinous.

In 1896 Gipps took the LSWR and GWR to the Railway and Canal Commissioners for restraint of trade. The hearings were lengthy and complex, but in the end Gipps got his way. The two larger companies had to grant through booking rates and timetables to freight from the DN&SR irrespective of where it had originated. Takings and profits rose again.

In 1901 Gipps displayed his business acumen in unexpected, but highly profitable, fashion. He travelled to Britanny and held talks with farmers and wholesalers of new potatoes. Back in England, he chartered the 80 ton steamer SS *Fred* for the months of May and June. When May came, the SS *Fred* docked at St Malo and loaded up with sacks of new potatoes. It spent the next two months shuttling back and forth between St Malo and Southampton, heavily laden with new potatoes. These were transferred at Southampton to DN&SR trucks, which then raced north to carry the French delicacies to towns and cities of the Midlands and North.

By 1905 the DN&SR had three ships – the *Fred*, *Puffin* and *Zillah* – working in the new potato run. The railway kept the profitable trade going right up to the outbreak of the Great War in 1914.

It was not just long-distance through freight that ran on the DN&SR. In the 1890s it was reckoned that each acre of arable farmland generated about a ton of freight of various kinds. The farms that stood close to the line would ship out their crops via the DN&SR, raising revenues accordingly. By 1913, before the Great War brought serious changes, the DN&SR was drawing 53% of its revenue from freight, 32% from passengers and 15% from local parcels and deliveries.

Throughout most of this period the passenger services remained at the rate of four per day. Though exact times varied, the first ran early in the morning, the second mid-morning, the third mid-afternoon and the final in the early evening. In 1883 the line added a passenger carriage to the rear of the freight train that left Newbury each weekday evening at 9.20 pm. This proved to be hugely popular with villagers who took advantage of it to have an evening out in town before heading home. Sadly, the Board of Trade stepped in to ban the service in 1892 when new regulations forbade such mixed trains.

In 1895 a new southbound train was instituted that left Didcot at 12.42 pm. This train missed the smaller rural stations and was advertised as a fast service to Winchester. It proved a success and in 1897 a through return train was introduced that left Southampton at 9.08 am, ran up the DN&SR to Didcot, then ran into Paddington to arrive at 11.45 am. It returned along the same route at 5.45 pm, reaching Southampton at 8.20 pm. In July 1901

A view of Didcot in 1915. The DN&SR trains used a bay platform on the south of the station, then ran east alongside the GWR lines for some distance before turning south.

yet another passenger service began, with the slipping of two coaches at Newbury from the 9.40 am Paddington–Weymouth express. These carriages were then run south along the DN&SR to Winchester, then joined to an LSWR train to Southampton. After 1903 carriages on the northbound early morning train were detached at Didcot and added to a train heading north to Newcastle.

By 1914 these various improvements meant that there were six trains in each direction running over the Berkshire section of the DN&SR. There was even a regular Sunday Summer Excursion. In 1913, the last full year of peace, the DN&SR sold well over 200,000 passenger tickets.

On 4 August 1914 Britain went to war with Germany. The DN&SR was never to be the same again. Less than 48 hours after the declaration of war, the government ordered the DN&SR to stop all its regular services. Instead the line was commandeered for use by the military. Troop trains and supply freight trains rattled back and forth with far greater frequency than the peacetime schedules had ever envisaged. The old rifle ranges at Churn, established by Loyd-Lindsay, were taken over by the army. The remote private station of Churn overnight became a busy army depot and a new platform had to be built. The area around Winchester became a major army camp used by regiments going to France, or by men returning on leave. Army specials serving these camps generated huge amounts of traffic on the line.

Profitable as all this was, the disruptions of wartime were, in fact, fatal to the DN&SR. The demands of the military meant that although civilian trains were reinstated, they were subject to delays and sudden cancellation at short notice. People and companies got out of the habit of using the DN&SR. By 1920, when the army camps were finally closed down, the DN&SR was running at a severe loss. In 1923 the company was bought by the GWR, most shareholders losing money on the deal.

Having acquired the DN&SR, the GWR does not seem to have known quite what to do with it. Little attempt was made to integrate the timetable to that of the GWR, nor did through trains become any more numerous. Nevertheless some improvements were made. In 1934 the turntable at Winchester was increased in size from 42 feet to 46 feet so that a wider variety of tender engines could work the route. Meanwhile, the GWR Duke class 4-4-0 engines had entered service on the line in the 1920s, proving themselves to be ideal for the route and remaining on the line to the 1940s.

The pressure of competition from buses and lorries increased dramatically in the 1920s and 1930s. By 1938 only four trains a day ran on what had been the DN&SR. Three ran from Didcot to Southampton, the fourth from Oxford to Southampton. Annual ticket sales were down to 56,000 and freight traffic was falling just as fast.

Then came the Second World War and again everything changed. This time, the former DN&SR line was not immediately commandeered, but instead was allowed to continue much as before, except for additional freight trains which ran along it to relieve pressure on the LSWR and GWR main lines, particularly after May 1940 when these began to be subjected to Luftwaffe bombing raids.

Then on 4 August 1942 the government ordered that the old DN&SR line was to be closed until further notice. No explanation was given, wartime secrecy being what it was. But there was no way the locals could miss the large gangs of workmen and heavy construction equipment that was soon at work along the line. The whole northern section of the old DN&SR route was being upgraded to dual track, as was much of the southern section. Moreover, the crossing loops were extended greatly in size, so that goods trains of over 70 wagons could use them. Platforms, signalling equipment and bridges were also improved.

Although only a select few knew it at the time, the former DN&SR line had been earmarked to be a major supply route for the US army divisions that would take part in the D-Day invasions of Normandy, due to take place in 1944. The works were completed by April 1943 and the line reopened. Although in theory the civilian traffic was now back to normal, in practice it took second place to the 45 or so military trains that used the line each day. As with the boom in traffic during the Great War, the increase in the years 1943–45 proved to be both temporary and destructive. The old DN&SR line was left with dual tracking that could not possibly be justified by the limited freight and passenger traffic that used the route when peace came in 1945.

In 1947 the line was nationalised, along with all others in Berkshire, to become part of the new British Railways. Despite the supposed advantages of consolidation, the Western Region continued to be run in just as isolated a fashion as had the GWR – but without the independent pride of that private company.

The section of line from Newbury to Didcot saw a temporary increase in freight traffic during the years 1947–55 as trains were diverted along the line to allow major maintenance and rebuilding on the main lines that had been so badly damaged or over-used during the war years. Meanwhile the regular trains on the line were by now being hauled by Dean 0-6-0 tender engines or Collett 0-6-0 taper boilers.

An 0-6-0 PT rests outside the depot in about 1955. (Courtesy of D. E. Canning)

Down Cornish Riviera runs into Newbury East Junction in 1960. The line curving away to the left is the Didcot-Newbury-Southampton line running north towards Didcot. (Courtesy of D. E. Canning)

In April 1961 the survey of rail traffic that would lead to the infamous Beeching Report, *The Reshaping of British Railways*, examined what had been the DN&SR line. It was found that the passenger traffic had virtually ceased to exist, as buses were offering a cheaper alternative. More encouragingly, freight traffic was averaging around 8,000 tons per week. However, it was predicted that this through freight traffic could be handled on other lines without undue problems.

The last passenger train on the southern section ran on 9 September 1961. The last passenger train on the Berkshire section ran from Didcot to Newbury on 8 September 1962. Freight traffic continued to the now unmanned stations until 10 August 1964, when the stations were closed and the line

On the downs just east of Chilton the DN&SR ran through a deep cutting that carried it up from Didcot to the high ground above. This is the southern end of the cutting where the railway ran out onto the open downland.

Almost a mile from the nearest road, the DN&SR built this impressive bridge over their cutting above Chilton to allow farmers to drive livestock from one area of downland grazing to another. The cutting on the far side has partially collapsed and the debris is now washing through the central arch.

relegated for use by through trains only. On 19 October 1967 the points joining the old DN&SR to the main line at Newbury were secured out of use. The rails were never used again.

Today, the impressive engineering works of the DN&SR means that there is much to see along the route of the old railway, though its often fairly remote location means that more effort is needed to find it. In Didcot the route of the line has been obliterated by modern building, but south of the town the embankment can be seen clearly marching up towards Upton. In Upton itself the old station is now a private house. A path that runs beside the welcoming George and Dragon pub heads south to go alongside the old railway route. This path gives

Ivy grows over the parapet of the bridge over the cutting near Chilton. Despite being untended for many decades, the brickwork is still largely secure and serves as a testament to the skills of those who built the DN&SR.

excellent views of the mighty cutting – now collapsing in places – carved out of the chalk south of Upton. Near Chilton stands a fine three-arched brick bridge over the cutting that may still be crossed on foot.

The railway station at Hampstead Norreys has been demolished to clear space for a modern housing estate, but the bridge that carried the road over the track survives. The route of the track is now followed by a footpath that links the new estate to the village.

South of the cutting, the route of the DN&SR runs over open downland that is privately owned and where public footpaths are absent. At Compton the line can be picked up again in the form of a cutting, although the old station has been completely demolished and its site is now occupied by a school. The station at Hampstead Norreys has likewise been demolished, though here a fine bridge remains and can be inspected at close quarters from a public footpath. South of Hampstead Norreys the line runs along an embankment beside the B4009, making the route easy to trace all the way down to Hermitage. The station here remains, but is a private house, and much of the land around it has been redeveloped for housing. South of the village the line

The station at Hermitage survives intact, but is now a private house at the end of a long drive and can be only glimpsed from the road.

of the tracks again runs beside the B4009 and is intermittently clearly visible. The line finally vanishes from modern view on the outskirts of Newbury.

5

The Coley Branch

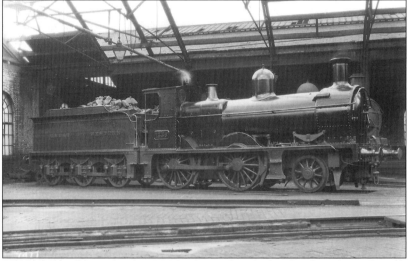

The 2-4-0 tender engine no 1336 in the engine shed at Reading Central goods depot.

When Isambard Kingdom Brunel, chief engineer of the Great Western Railway was selecting the route to carry his railway west past Reading he chose to put the tracks on the north side of the town. In the 1830s the decision made sense, but was later to cause problems that were solved only by the construction of the Coley branch.

By putting the tracks north of the town, Brunel was able to take advantage of the relatively flat land that bordered the River Thames, making construction both cheap and easy. He was also able to put the station for Reading facing onto the main road (now the A32) that ran down from the town to cross the Thames by the bridge at Caversham, while still keeping it close to the main London–Bristol road (now the A4). This made the station ideally placed to take advantage of trade from passengers whether they were heading for Reading itself, places north of the Thames or places further west up the valley of the Kennet.

What had not been foreseen as clearly as it might have been was the enormous boost to industry and trade that the railway gave to Reading. This growth in prosperity and population became even greater after the GWR added a branch running from Reading to Newbury and Hungerford in 1847 and another to Basingstoke in 1848. These branches were served by a new station, Reading West, on the outskirts of the town. By 1860 Reading was more than twice the size of Abingdon, which until 1830 had been the larger town.

This boom in industry led to a massive increase in freight traffic along the GWR, far more than Brunel had envisaged. By the 1890s the situation was getting out of hand. The facilities in the goods yard at Reading station and at Reading West simply

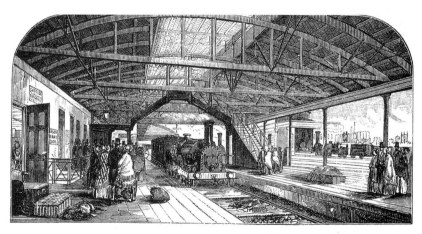

THE READING STATION.

The original GWR Reading station in 1852. It was to relieve pressure on the freight yard at this station that the Coley branch was built. (Taken from The Illustrated Guide to the Great Western Railway *by George Meason, 1852)*

could not cope, nor could the goods yard at the SER station of Reading Southern, built adjacent to the GWR yards at Reading station. The townsfolk of Reading were none too pleased either by the seemingly unending stream of carts and drays making their way up and down the slope from the stations into the town centre. Jams were frequent, while enormous nuisance was caused by horse droppings, wheels rumbling over cobbles and the occasional upset.

Clearly what was needed, the senior officials of the GWR believed, was a spur rail line dedicated to freight only that ran into the very centre of Reading. The problem was where to put it without the need to demolish half the town. The answer came in the unlikely form of the Reading Masonic Lodge Hall. This large and imposing building fronted onto the town centre and backed onto the floodplain of the River Kennet. Just north of the site the stream was hemmed in by flood-proof banks as it ran through the town centre but, south and west of the Masonic Hall, the river ran through wide meadows, which flooded frequently in wet weather. Unwelcoming as this marshy ground might seem, it did provide a route from the Newbury branch of the GWR right into the centre of Reading without the need to demolish any buildings, except the Masonic Hall.

The GWR engineers got to work surveying a route from the Newbury branch, round the southern edge of Coley Park, the grounds of a prestigious manor on the south-western edge of the town, and over the Kennet watermeadows. Finally the Great Western Railway (Additional Powers) Act was passed by Parliament on 4 August 1905. The new line was to be just less than two miles long, though its construction would require much in the way of land drainage, embankment construction and bridging. The Masonic Hall was bought and demolished, a new hall being built at GWR expense elsewhere in the town.

The line from the Newbury branch to the goods yard was single track, though it became double track just before it reached the main GWR rails to facilitate safer switching. Where the line ran alongside the River Kennet for a short stretch, three sidings were constructed to reach the river at Bear Wharf. Here goods

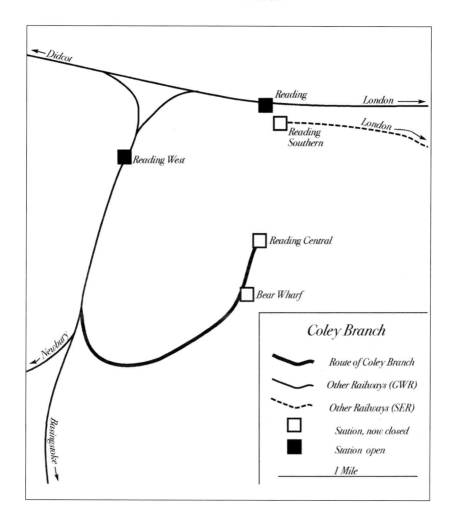

could be transferred from rail to barge, or vice versa. Beyond Bear Wharf the line reverted to single track before suddenly dividing into six pairs of parallel sidings in the goods yard itself. Each pair of sidings had its own set of cranes, platforms and links into the town via the site of the now demolished Masonic Hall and into Berkeley Avenue.

The new line and goods yard opened on 4 May 1908 and was immediately busy. Coal was, as so often at this date, the main bulk freight being passed through the yard, but brick, stone, hay and straw were not far behind.

So successful was the yard and its branch line at bringing freight into Reading, that it was not long before other companies decided to take advantage. The Co-operative Society had a jam factory in Reading that was handling such quantities of fruit and sugar that the company built its own siding in the Reading Central goods yard. The H & G Simonds brewery followed suit to bring barley and hops to their premises and to ship ale out again. Nor were they alone as the Anglo-American Oil Company (now part of Esso) likewise constructed its own sidings, as did Baynes Timber Merchants.

Busy as it was, the yard was not without its problems. The line out of the yard towards the main line at Coley was restricted to a speed of just 15 mph, and only one train in steam was allowed at any one time. The speed limit was later raised to 30 mph after a few improvements had been made.

Rather more long-term was the lack of a water supply. When the yard had first been planned it was felt that this would not be a problem. It was soon realised, however, that the yard was so busy that a tank engine could not carry enough water for a full day's work. Tender engines had to be brought in to shunt the wagons around. The 2251 class 0-6-0 engines were often used, though later the BR 2-6-0 Standard class 4 were more usual.

Thriving as the goods yard and its branch line were, they could not keep up with the pace of change. Coal freight dwindled dramatically as houses converted to gas or electric heating and ovens. The hay and straw trade collapsed as motor vehicles replaced horse-drawn carts and buses. Increasingly general goods were being transported by road.

By 1956 the amount of freight being handled had fallen dramatically. The double tracks at the junction with the main line were replaced with a single junction to the down line. This meant that up trains leaving the branch had to run over the down line in the wrong direction for a short distance before switching to the up line. In the yard's heyday this would have

Reading station photographed in 1968. The building with a squat tower sporting two arched windows is the old GWR station. The LSWR station has been demolished, but was formerly on the site occupied in this photo by the car park. (Courtesy of D.E. Canning)

been both too dangerous and would have imposed too many delays on main line trains to even contemplate. But with the numbers of trains falling it was considered safe and convenient.

Another blow came in September 1964 when the Co-op switched all their freight to road. The Co-op sidings were taken up. Five years later Bear Wharf was closed down, and again the sidings serving it were removed. Finally the goods yard was

The site of the Reading Central goods depot photographed in 2006. The dual carriageway is the A33 and warehousing stands on either side. No trace of the station remains.

closed down entirely on 25 July 1983. By January 1985 the rails had been lifted and the junction with the main line was removed.

Today, the goods yard has been totally obliterated. Its site is now covered by the roundabout, flyover and underpass of the junction between the A4, A33 and A327. To the south, the A33 follows the route of the old branch line past Bear Wharf, now likewise totally destroyed, after which it runs south towards the M3, M4 and Basingstoke.

There are, however, some traces of the old branch line to be found. The bridge over the River Kennet remains, as do the embankments that lead up to it from either side. These can be accessed by a footpath from Yew Lane, part of the modern housing estate that has now been built over what was the prestigious Coley Park when the branch line was first built. Although the actual junction with the main line has been removed, the flat area where it once stood is still in place, just at the southern end of the cutting that carries the line south of Reading West station. There is a footpath across this land, but it is difficult to find. However, the area can be seen quite clearly from passing trains.

6
The Regatta Line

A 4-6-0 tender engine hauls a passenger train past Twyford East signal box. The points for a right turn to Henley are situated about 25 yards in front of it.

The busy, thriving town of Henley was a prosperous river port in the 1830s, so the citizens were probably relieved rather than upset to be bypassed by the new Great Western Railway.

Isambard Kingdom Brunel laid out a route for the GWR that ran direct from Maidenhead to Reading. This meant cutting through the hill at Sonning, a major feat of engineering, but if the flat land along the river had been followed, the route would have many miles longer. Quite soon the fast, modern railway was taking traffic off the riverboats. In the first year that the GWR ran, the boats lost 23% of their trade and by 1845 long-distance traffic had effectively ceased to operate on the Thames.

Henley was left with only local river transport, and its docks and warehouses stood empty. Moreover, the town council watched with envious eyes as Reading prospered on goods brought in by rail. Factories, breweries and mills boomed in Reading, but faded in Henley.

In the spring of 1854, therefore, the Mayor of Henley led a delegation to the offices of the Great Western Railway in London. The townsfolk asked the company to open a branch line to Henley. The GWR had already surveyed a route from Twyford to Henley, but had not gone ahead with the line due to worries about its ability to turn a profit in the face of local hostility. Now that the town council and leading citizens were fully behind the plan, the financial sums were very different. Construction work began that autumn under the direction of a GWR engineer called Murray.

The route to be taken was uniformly flat and free of obstructions, except for one: the Thames. The site chosen for the crossing was just downstream of Shiplake Lock where an island provided a convenient base for the bridge piers in midstream. Murray decided that the budget he had been given would not stretch to a proper bridge, so a timber viaduct was constructed to carry the railway over the river. By this date the Thames Commissioners, who organised river trade and kept the river navigable, were teetering on the edge of bankruptcy with debts of around £50,000. They were in no position to insist on keeping the river clear for large boats, so Murray's viaduct gave clearance for only smaller barges such as made up the vast majority of the local river trade.

After taking a surprisingly sharp bend as it left Twyford, the branch line ran almost directly north to cross the river, then bent slightly to the west to run into Henley. Murray built just two stations on the five mile length. The first was slightly north of the river crossing at Shiplake, which consisted of little more than a platform and a lockable shed. The station at Henley was grander, having a proper station building in the GWR style and an engine shed.

On 1 June 1857 the new line opened with a public breakfast at Henley Town Hall. Over 70 people attended, among them

TWYFORD STATION

Twyford station before the branch line was constructed. This view is looking to the west, so the branch line would later be built to turn off right beyond the station building. (Taken from The Illustrated Guide to the Great Western Railway *by George Meason, 1852)*

This undated photograph of Twyford station appears to be from the 1890s, judging by the flat-topped peaked caps worn by the station staff. The small tank engine visible on the left of the picture is on the branch line. On the right is Twyford West signal box.

Henley station in 1919. This view is taken looking towards the town along the passenger platforms. The goods yard lies to the left, mostly out of view.

Murray, the Mayor and several directors of the GWR. There were to be five trains each way each day, with four on Sundays – a respectable service for a branch line.

The service was not so frequent that Murray had thought the installation of signals to be necessary. Instead there were two Line Constables on duty. The shelter of the first, at Ruscombe, was the only building on the railway in the Berkshire section south of the Thames. This shelter resembled a sentry box mounted on a swivel platform that enabled the Constable within to move it round so that the back was kept to the wind and rain.

The Constable had the task of keeping a note of which trains had passed him in which direction and when the next was to be expected. When a train came into sight, the Constable had to leave his shelter and stand beside the track to give one of three signals. The 'Clear' signal involved facing the track and holding the right arm straight out, parallel to the ground. This meant

The Henley branch acquired standard GWR signals soon after it was opened. Introduced in 1840 and serving to the 1880s, these bar and disc signals stood on 40 foot poles. When the disc, carrying a white light at night, faced oncoming trains it showed the line was clear ahead. If the signal swivelled so that the bar, carrying a red light at night, faced the train it indicated danger. The signals were designed to be visible up to five miles distant. The bar on this signal has no tail, so it is from an up line. (Courtesy Didcot Railway Centre)

that no other trains were on the line. The 'Caution' signal was given by facing the oncoming train and lifting the right arm up over the head. This meant that the route ahead was thought to be clear, but that another train was on the line so the train should proceed more slowly and with the driver keeping a close watch. The 'Danger' signal involved the Constable facing the oncoming train with both arms raised and the legs splayed out so that his body formed an X shape. This meant the train should stop so that the Constable could give the driver a message as to the state of the line or of expected trains. Because their work involved them being out in all weathers, the Constables were provided with a smart uniform in thick wool twill and a waterproof top hat.

It was not until the 1870s, that the Henley branch gained the semaphore signals that were by then becoming standard on the nation's railways. That same decade saw another change come to the branch. The broad gauge on which the GWR had been built was being abandoned in favour of the standard gauge used on all other rail lines. On the afternoon of Friday, 24 March 1876 special trains brought almost a thousand workmen and a vast array of tools and equipment to the line.

As the last evening train puffed by, the men went to work. The line was torn up and realigned on the standard gauge, with the ballast being repacked completely. The work was finished by the time the first morning train was ready to travel the branch line. The efficiency of the workmen and officials of the GWR was famous and this incident puts to shame the months-long work that blights rail lines and roadworks in the early 21st century.

In 1898 it was decided to make the branch line double tracked along its entire length. This work was made necessary by the congestion and confusion caused on the branch line each year by the Henley Regatta. Now that the town was no longer a working river port, the leisure potential of the river had become clear. Numbers attending the Regatta had boomed during the 1870s and 1880s as boating became a fashionable leisure and sporting activity.

During Regatta Week dozens of extra trains were laid on from Twyford to Henley, all decorated with flags, sculls and other

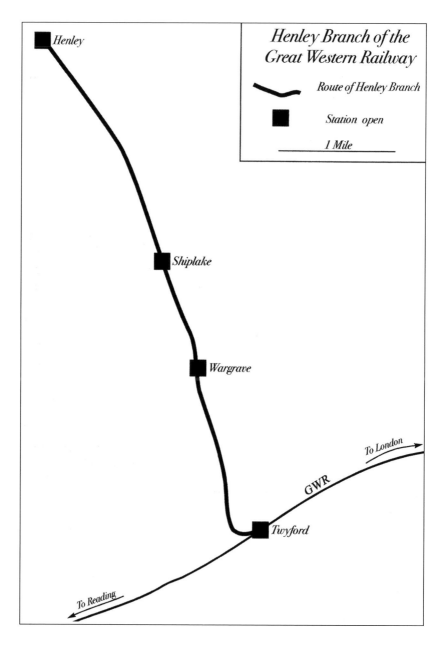

festive devices. So many trains and carriages packed the sidings that the GWR had to draft in dozens of extra staff to cope. The nine men regularly employed at Henley, and the lone men at Shiplake and Wargrave, more than had their hands full. Inevitably the temporary staff had to sleep somewhere and the GWR was unwilling to pay the costs of rooms during Regatta Week, even if they could be found. Instead a dining saloon and pair of coaches were pushed into the sidings for use by the staff. Secondment to Henley for Regatta Week became a much-coveted role for GWR staff due to the 'extensive jollifications' indulged in by the staff after the last train had left.

The introduction of double tracking gave the GWR the opportunity to build a new station at Wargrave, on the Berkshire section of the line. The new station had two platforms, each 500 feet long, with a standard single-storey brick GWR station building, with a wooden canopy over the platform, on the up side. A pair of lockable storage sheds was added later for parcels, bicycles and the like.

Once the line had been converted, a new timetable was introduced. This saw three through trains from Henley to Paddington run in each direction daily. A further through service down the line was provided by slipping a coach off the South Wales Mail at Twyford and attaching it to a branch train. There were five of these in each direction daily running from Twyford to Henley.

The branch engine was kept at Henley and was a Metro 2-4-0 tank engine, later replaced by a 57xx or 8750 class 0-6-0 pannier tank engine. These pulled two coaches plus a bogie brake third. The GWR, and later British Railways, often ran other engines on the route as the needs of the network dictated, so the Henley branch saw a more varied mix of engines than did most others. The through trains were hauled by a variety of tender engines, often a 4-6-0, though the larger Castle and King class engines were not allowed on the line due to their great axle weight.

In 1906 a small piece of railway history was made on the Henley branch line. The GWR Signal Department Works at Reading had been experimenting with ways to make signalling safer and more efficient. One key point that had been raised was

An 0-6-0 pannier tank engine waits at Henley ready to run up to Twyford. A 57xx or 8750 class tank engine was kept at Henley to work the shuttle passenger trains until 1958 when diesel engines arrived on the branch line.

that drivers and firemen were sometimes distracted by events in the cab, or unsighted by fog or smoke and so missed seeing some signals. In 1900 a nasty accident had occurred on the Windsor branch line when a driver missed a signal in fog. It was decided that a way should be found to link the visible trackside signals to an audible signal inside the cab.

It was in January 1906 that a trial system was introduced to the Henley line. The system worked by having a sloping metal shoe mounted on a wooden bar and placed between the two tracks. This metal shoe was connected to the signal so that it carried a small electric charge when the signal was set to 'Clear', but did not when the signal was at 'Caution' or 'Danger'. The engine was equipped with a metal flap under the cab that was

94

By 1958, when this photograph was taken, British Rail had replaced all the old GWR signs with new ones in their own corporate design. At this date the station received both diesel shuttle trains to Twyford and steam powered through trains to Paddington.

The lost station of Wargrave as it was in its heyday. The two tracks are still in place, while the original GWR station and canopies stand proudly. This view is looking towards Henley.

A similar view taken in 2006 shows that the main station buildings have been demolished and replaced with a simple metal shelter and noticeboard. A ticket machine has replaced the stationmaster. The footbridge has been removed as there is now only one platform and one track.

Wargrave station today. The tracks lie along the course of the original up line. The down trackbed still exists and can be seen as the level ground in the centre of the picture. During the demolition of the 1980s the concrete blocks that faced the down platform were removed, leaving only the rubble core of the platform. The bank to the right of the picture, now overgrown with trees and scrub, is all that remains of this platform.

pushed up when the engine passed over the metal shoe. If the shoe was electrified, the flap completed a circuit to a small electric bell in the cab that then rang briefly. If the shoe was not electrified, the flap instead set off a whistle that sounded continuously until the driver switched it off. Thus the footplate crew would know if a signal had been at 'Clear' or not, even if they had not seen it.

The experiment on the Henley branch was so successful that the GWR extended the trial to the main line between Slough and Reading in 1908. Two years later the innovation was installed throughout the GWR. Similar systems have since been adopted on almost all railways around the world.

In 1958 the pannier tanks were replaced by diesels for the branch trains, though steam tender engines continued to haul the through trains until 1963. By that time the branch line had been reduced once again to a single track. Freight services to Wargrave and Shiplake were scrapped in 1964 and the following year the stations lost their permanent staff. In the 1980s the old GWR brick-built station at Wargrave was demolished as it was becoming expensive to maintain and was no longer needed since neither goods nor parcels were any longer handled at the station that now had no staff. A bus shelter type of building was erected with automatic ticket machines.

Today the branch line still operates and is a thriving concern with 24 trains running in each direction daily. The bulk of the traffic is commuters travelling to work in London, though some local passengers also use the service. It was the old down line that was removed throughout when the branch became single tracked. The roadway was left intact, but has not been maintained. It is now so overgrown with bushes and increasingly mature trees that it is almost impossible to tell that this was once a double tracked line.

7

The Cookham Link

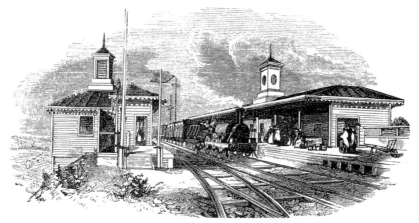

MAIDENHEAD STATION,

The original GWR Maidenhead station was built entirely of wood as it stood on top of an embankment where a light weight was essential. (Taken from The Illustrated Guide to the Great Western Railway *by George Meason, 1852)*

What is now the branch line from Maidenhead to Marlow, by way of Cookham, has had a chequered and patchy history. These days it is enjoying something of an upswing even though the original purpose of the line was long since made redundant by the closure of part of the line.

It was on 27 July 1846 that Parliament approved the Wycombe Railway Act, which envisaged a route running from Oxford to Maidenhead by way of Thame and High Wycombe with a branch line out to Aylesbury. Almost at once the company announced that it had failed to raise the necessary money to build the line. Nothing much happened for another six years, when the Wycombe Railway Company announced that it had hired as Chief Engineer none other than Isambard Kingdom Brunel, the greatest engineer of his age and mastermind of the Great Western Railway. Brunel had agreed to work for the Wycombe Railway Company only on condition that he was allowed a completely free hand in the design of the railway and its works. The directors were only too pleased to agree so long as their relatively minor project got the name of Brunel associated with it.

As hoped, the arrival of the new engineer led to a change in fortunes. Construction work began, although there was only enough money to get the line from Maidenhead as far as High Wycombe. Brunel insisted on a number of special features for the new railway. The first was that it should be built to his preferred broad gauge of 7 feet ¼ inch, rather than the standard gauge of 4 feet 8½ inches. The broad gauge was that used on the GWR, though other railways had preferred the standard gauge.

A second stipulation was that, apart from the main station at Wycombe, all the stations had to be constructed to an identical design. These were to have a booking office at one end with an open porch or waiting area at the other. Stations that had a level crossing beside them were provided with a small house in which the crossing keeper could live. The buildings were all to be of brick and knapped flint. Brunel believed this design incorporated everything a smaller station would need, while the standardisation would help to keep costs down.

It was the third decision that was to cause trouble. Brunel always had a liking for innovative design and for the tracks he chose the new and impressive, but untried, Barlow rails. These had been invented by William Henry Barlow, Chief Engineer to the Midland Railway, and were being used on all the lines running out of St Pancras.

The exciting feature of the Barlow rails was that they did not need sleepers. Instead of being tied to timbers at frequent intervals to keep them in position, the Barlow rails relied on inertia. They took the form of an upside down V, the hollow centre being packed with sand and gravel before the rail was buried half deep in the ballast of the road bed. The technique speeded up construction and made it easier to lay out complex

A section of Barlow rails, as originally used on the Cookham line. These rails did not need sleepers. Note the wide flanged base that was buried in the ballast to provide stability. (Courtesy of the Didcot Railway Centre)

patterns of crossovers and points. Experience was to show that the rails were not as stable in the long term as Barlow and Brunel had hoped, but that was for the future.

In the 1850s all seemed well for the new Wycombe Railway. Construction was completed quickly and efficiently under Brunel's watchful eye. On 1 August 1854 the line was opened from Maidenhead to High Wycombe. There then followed a pause to raise more capital before the line was pushed on to reach Thame in August 1862, Aylesbury in October 1863 and finally Oxford in October 1864.

The Berkshire section of the Wycombe Railway was only ever a small part of its total length. From a junction with the GWR at Maidenhead, the line curved sharply north, then ran gently downhill to the station at Cookham. It continued downhill to reach the damp, boggy watermeadows of Cock Marsh. These

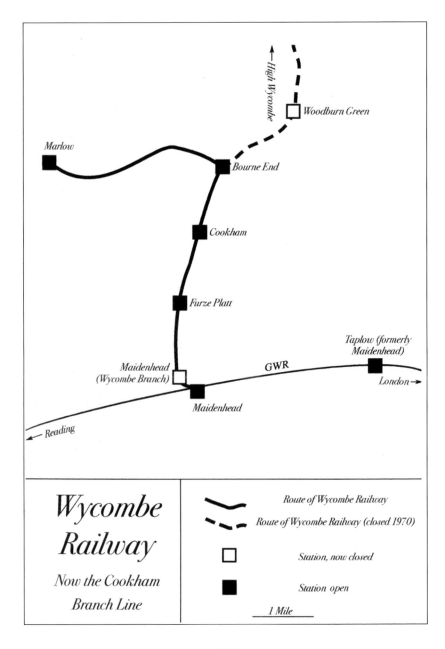

Marlow

Woodburn Green

Bourne End

Cookham

Furze Platt

Taplow (formerly
Maidenhead)

Maidenhead
(Wycombe Branch)

GWR

London →

Maidenhead

← Reading

*Wycombe
Railway*

Now the Cookham
Branch Line

Route of Wycombe Railway

Route of Wycombe Railway (closed 1970)

Station, now closed

Station open

1 Mile

Taken in about 1912 this photo of Cookham shows a variety of road transport as well as the Metro 2-4-0 tank waiting at the down platform. (Courtesy of Lens of Sutton)

were crossed by a low viaduct, later replaced by an embankment. The line then crossed the Thames by way of a wooden viaduct, later replaced by an iron girder bridge. It entered Bourne End station before running on through Woodburn Green to Loudwater and so to High Wycombe.

Having overseen the successful construction of the line, the Wycombe Railway Company decided to take a backseat when it came actually to running the trains. The line was leased out to the GWR, which ran it profitably until 1867 when the GWR bought out the Wycombe Railway Company.

Having bought the company, the GWR made three significant changes. The first was made in 1870 when the line was closed for seven days in August. During that time the Barlow rails were taken out and the line converted along its entire length to standard gauge track using conventional tracks laid on sleepers.

The second change made by the GWR was to alter the timetable and operation of the Wycombe line so that it became effectively two distinct branch lines. The line from Maidenhead to High Wycombe was operated by trains shuttling back and forth.

The third change imposed by the GWR affected not just the Wycombe line, but also the GWR main line itself. When the GWR had been driven through Maidenhead in 1838 the company had acquired land adjacent to what is now the A4, to the east of the town, for its station. This site was inconvenient for a number of reasons, not least the fact that it was on the opposite side of the Thames from the town, and the owners of the bridge charged a toll for its use. Moreover, the fact that the station stood

The 61 6106 pulls a passenger train out of Taplow in 1970. What is now Taplow was the original Maidenhead station and for some time was the western terminus of the Great Western Railway from London. It was renamed Taplow on 1 May 1869 as the current Maidenhead station was being built. (Courtesy of D. E. Canning)

104

All that remains of the original Maidenhead station on the Cookham line is this bricked up archway beside Castle Hill, just west of the town centre. The station buildings behind have long since been demolished.

105

A train pulls into Furze Platt today. The station never consisted of more than a single platform with a simple shelter for passengers. The original wooden shed shelter was removed in the 1980s to be replaced by the current metal and glass affair.

on an embankment forced Brunel to build a station of wood, rather than the more imposing brick or stone that a town such as Maidenhead would normally have been granted. As early as 1838 the board of the GWR passed a motion authorising Maidenhead station to be moved to a new site further west, but nothing was done.

When Brunel was designing the Wycombe Railway he inserted a station adjacent to the town centre almost immediately after the new line diverged from that of the GWR. This new station was built to the standard design for smaller Wycombe stations, but was ideally positioned for passengers from Maidenhead. Because the line was leased to the GWR, passengers were able to buy through tickets from the new Maidenhead (Wycombe branch) station to any station on the GWR network. The new station thrived while the supposedly main line Maidenhead station became something of a backwater.

The GWR did not relish running two stations, especially with the busier of the two being on a branch line. As soon as the larger company acquired the smaller it was decided to rationalise the situation. A site was acquired immediately to the east of the junction of the two lines and construction of a new, imposing station to GWR design began. The new station was opened on 1 November 1871, and the old Wycombe line station closed next day. Meanwhile the old main line station was rebuilt and renamed Taplow.

The layout remained unaltered until 1937. The population of Maidenhead had been increasing steadily over the years and by the 1930s extensive suburbs had been built to the north and

An 0-6-0 T waits at Bourne End while passengers board. This train is heading towards Maidenhead. (Courtesy of D. E. Canning)

107

The station at Cookham retains the neat brick and flint building erected by Brunel. The brick-only section is a modern extension housing a business unrelated to the railways.

west. On 5 July 1937 a station was opened at Furze Platt to cater for the new residents who wanted to travel from their homes to work or play without the bother of a long walk or bus ride to reach a train. The station was at first simply a low wooden platform with a wooden shed serving as a waiting room. This was later replaced by a higher and more robust concrete platform and a bus shelter style construction in which passengers could huddle in inclement weather.

On 4 May 1970 the line between Bourne End and High Wycombe was closed. The passing loop at Cookham was removed, as was the double track junction with the main line at Maidenhead. The branch line became single track throughout.

Today the line operates as a shuttle between Maidenhead and Marlow with over 20 trains in each direction daily. The old

A view of Cookham railway station looking towards Maidenhead today. The single line occupies the position of the old up line. The position of the original down line is now a mere flat area of ballast. The facing of the old down platform has been retained and separates the modern car park from the track. The iron railings formerly ran at the back of the platform, but have been moved to further separate the car park from the track.

109

Maidenhead station that was closed in the 1870s has long since vanished, but its entrance still stands in awkward isolation beside the A4 just outside Maidenhead town centre.

The station at Cookham is not so very different from how it looked in Brunel's day, though there have been some changes. A glazed footbridge has been erected and then removed, while the lighting system is now provided by modern, high-level electric lights instead of the original oil lanterns. The main station building is little altered, apart from some ugly 1960s windows. The entire Berkshire length of the line can still be travelled.

8
The Royal Trains

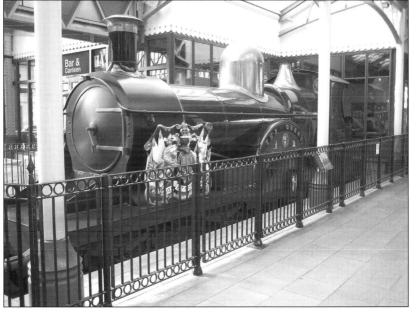

Standing forlorn and isolated in what is now a shopping arcade, the old GWR locomotive 'The Queen' formerly occupied pride of place in an exhibition about royalty and the railways at Windsor.

Only one branch line was originally envisaged for the Great Western Railway when plans were being drawn up in the 1830s, that from Slough to Windsor. Ironically, it was the short branch line rather than the longer main line that was to cause the directors of the GWR the most headaches and take longest to bring into service.

The town council at Windsor was annoyed that the GWR had abandoned an early proposal for the main line to run through

Windsor, due to engineering considerations. They also recognised that if the railway came to Windsor the coaching trade would decline, leaving the council without the revenues generated by 80 coaches a day paying the bridge toll. Such a loss of revenue might have been acceptable if the main line rails came through Windsor, but not for the sake of a mere branch. The council decided to oppose the GWR Bill then in Parliament.

Eton, meanwhile, opposed the whole idea of a railway on principle. In January 1834 Dr Keane, the headmaster of Eton College, spoke to a public meeting in Windsor Guildhall, announcing: 'It will be impossible to keep the boys from the railroad in their hours of liberty. I cannot help thinking that it will very materially endanger the discipline of the school.' He even went so far a few days later as to suggest that his boys might 'do that which will occasion great danger to the passengers out of playfulness'.

Faced by such opposition, the promoters of the GWR Bill accepted an amendment that dropped the Windsor branch line. The idea was, however, not forgotten. In purchasing land at Slough, provision was made for the future path of a branch line heading towards Windsor.

Meanwhile, the Windsor council had given support to the newly formed London and Windsor Railway Company, which aimed to build a line from the capital to Windsor by way of Osterley as the first stage of a much grander route down to the south-west of England. A key problem was that the route envisaged crossing royal lands. King William IV was consulted and gave his permission for a line to be built over the Home Park so that it entered the town by way of Datchet Lane.

Eton, as ever, opposed the construction of a railway anywhere near the college. The influence exercised by the college on peers of the realm, together with growing worries over the financial stability of the project, ensured that the London and Windsor Railway Bill was defeated in the House of Lords.

The GWR promptly put forward a new Bill to Parliament seeking permission for its own branch line to be constructed along roughly the same lines as previously envisaged. Eton objected again, though a newly elected council at Windsor did not. The Bill was passed by Parliament, but only after Thomas Carter, Provost of Eton, had managed to get so many restrictions and conditions imposed that the GWR judged the project to be commercially unviable. Once again the branch line idea was dropped.

Nevertheless, there were obvious commercial prospects for a railway to Windsor. In October 1845 a 14 day period showed the following traffic over the toll bridge across the Thames:

Pedestrians	353,998
Private vehicles and riders	90,806
Post riders	63,022
Passengers on omnibus	140,785

At an average of some 46,300 paying customers each day, if a railway was able to capture even a part of this market, there would be much money to be made.

In August 1845 the Windsor, Slough and Staines Atmospheric Railway Company was formed. This aimed to build a line from Slough, through Windsor to Staines. It hoped to get around the opposition of Eton by building in a wide curve to the west of the college. The company hoped to overcome objections now emanating from the Crown authorities about noise, nuisance and dirt, for which the early engines of this period were notorious, by adopting the atmospheric system pioneered by Brunel on a short line in Devon.

The atmospheric system was ingenious. It relied on an iron tube laid between the two tracks. A rod from the train projected down and into the tube, where it ended in an airtight piston. At either end of the line, or at intervals along it if it were a long line, were erected massive stationary steam engines inside large buildings. These maintained high air pressure inside the iron tubes, which pushed the trains along by way of the piston. Speeds of up to 60 mph were reached on the line in Devon.

Unfortunately by the time the Bill came before Parliament in May 1845 two major problems had arisen. The first was that the Devon line had shown the atmospheric system to be almost unusable in hot, dry weather as the leather seals dried out and

113

cracked. Second, the Crown refused permission for the line to cross royal lands. The opposition of Eton was still vociferous, but was now almost taken for granted. The Bill was voted down in May 1846.

With commendable perseverance the GWR stepped forward yet again, buying out the shareholders of the atmospheric railway company and again promoting its branch line from Slough. This time they met opposition from a fresh quarter: the London and South Western Railway. The LSWR proposed a route from its line at Staines along that which had been proposed by the atmospheric railway.

Stormy meetings took place in Windsor as the public debated the merits of the rival proposals. Allegations were made that the GWR had lent their navvies smart clothes and sent them to pack the meetings, while GWR backers countered that the LSWR were distributing bribes in Parliament. The press had a field day as the disputes spilled into Parliament and threatened to touch the Crown itself.

In May 1847 Parliament chose to turn down the GWR line and instead give permission to the LSWR proposal, but only so far as Datchet. There was still to be no railway to Windsor.

One result of the bitter battle between the GWR and LSWR was that Queen Victoria and Prince Albert made it very clear to all concerned, and to the public, that they had absolutely no view on the matter at all. The business of a railway to Windsor was entirely in the hands of the Commissioners who managed the Windsor Estates. This led to the curious situation where eminent men on all sides voiced views as to what was convenient for Her Majesty, or what was inconvenient, with absolutely no way of finding out what the Queen thought herself.

This gave the railway companies their chance. The Commissioners were known to be keen to make dramatic improvements to the castle and its surroundings to benefit the Royal Family and to make a visit more impressive for foreign heads of state. They were also known to have virtually no money to pay for the desired works. It was the GWR that first suggested that it might be willing to make donations to help

Seen from the western end of the platform a 61XX class 2-6-2 tank engine prepares to haul a passenger train out of Windsor and Eton Central in 1958. (Courtesy of Lens of Sutton)

fund the work in return for the Commissioners' support and permission for its line. The Commissioners took up the idea with enthusiasm, and promptly entered into similar negotiations with the LSWR.

The talks between the Crown Commissioners and the two railway companies dragged on for months and were complicated, as ever, by Eton College as well as by the views of various men of note in Parliament. Eventually the Commissioners managed to get the then enormous sum of £85,000 from the two companies. In return, the Commissioners agreed to allow through what was, in effect, a variation on the plans of the atmospheric railway route. The GWR was to build a branch on the revised route from Slough to Windsor; the LSWR would follow the route from Windsor to Staines.

That left only Eton College to be won over. The GWR agreed to screen the river bathing places used by the college from the railway, to provide a place for a man from the college to be on duty at the station to stop boys absconding and masters would be given concessionary travel. Even so, the college remained adamantly opposed, but its supporters in Parliament felt unable to vote down the line given the compromise offered by the GWR.

On 14 August 1848 Parliamentary permission was at last given for the railways to reach Windsor. The parish church at Windsor rang a celebratory peal of bells.

The GWR had begun work even before the final vote and speed was considered vital. Teams of navvies were put to work night and day, and every sort of comfort was provided in the camps so that the men were not tempted to the towns of Slough or Windsor. There was even a temporary church made of canvas and wood. The first casualty came in March when a 17 year old navvy named George Norman broke his arm. More serious was the accident that September when Joseph Moyser, a riveter, fell into the Thames while working on the bridge and drowned.

The engineering works needed by the GWR were formidable. Not only did the Thames have to be bridged, but cuttings and embankments had to be constructed to carry the branch line out of Slough. To speed things up it was decided to cross the broad watermeadows around the Thames by way of a timber viaduct. And once past the meadows there was a steep incline up to Windsor that needed to be levelled off. Finally most of George Street had to be demolished to make way for the station and sidings.

One of the key problems proved to be the bridge over the Thames. A two-span arch with a pier in midstream was the first design put forward by the GWR. Eton College, however, successfully argued that this would make boating virtually impossible, so Parliament insisted that a single span bridge be erected. Brunel was, as ever, equal to the challenge. He designed a wrought-iron bridge of the 'arch and tie' design that weighed 450 tons. It was manufactured in sections elsewhere, brought by

Brunel's iron bridge over the Thames is the oldest of the master engineer's metal bridges to remain intact.

rail to the Thames and assembled on site. This bridge is the oldest of Brunel's metal bridges to remain intact.

By May 1849 it looked as if the GWR might open its line first. The directors of the LSWR knew that their line had further to go, but had assumed that the lack of any real engineering, other than a bridge over the Thames, would mean they would get to Windsor first. Now they dragged their Chief Engineer for the line, Joseph Locke, to a meeting and demanded that he and his men work faster. To save time, Locke decided to rest his bridge on a pier that was made of cast-iron cylinders in the centre of the riverbed, instead of the more traditional stone, built within a coffer dam. It proved to be an expensive mistake.

The LSWR line was completed in the first week of August. The LSWR sent for the government inspector to view the line, rolling stock and engines to give his permission to open to the public.

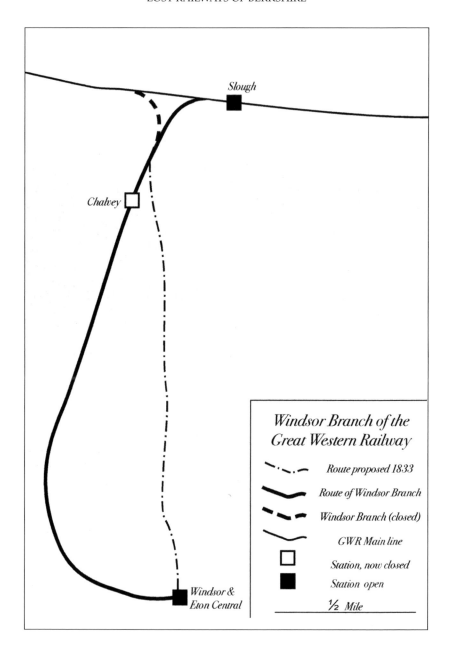

Slough

Chalvey

Windsor Branch of the
Great Western Railway

— ·· — Route proposed 1833

▬▬ Route of Windsor Branch

▬ ▬ Windsor Branch (closed)

⌐ GWR Main line

☐ Station, now closed

■ Station open

½ Mile

Windsor &
Eton Central

A modern electric train crosses the former LSWR bridge over the Thames on its way from Windsor to London. It was the sudden collapse of the original bridge on this site that caused the LSWR to lose the race with the GWR to be the first to open a branch line to Windsor.

He was due to arrive on 15 August, but on 14 August one of the cast-iron cylinders gave way, causing the girders supporting the rail tracks to shift and break. At once the bridge was torn down and work began on a replacement, but it was too late.

On 8 October the official opening of the GWR line into Windsor took place. The first train left Slough at 8.05 am and arrived at 8.11 am. The first through train from London Paddington arrived at 8.30 am. The LSWR line opened on 1 December, when a train departed for London Waterloo at 8.10 am.

Queen Victoria left Windsor by train for the first time on 23 November 1849. Her carriage was escorted down to the GWR station by a party from the Grenadier Guards while the

The main building of the LSWR station. This is the second station to stand on the site, the earlier building having been a temporary wooden affair.

GWR provided a brass band to play the national anthem. Brunel was in attendance, along with GWR directors Charles Russell, Charles Saunders and Daniel Gooch. Gooch took the controls and drove the train to Slough.

Both companies had cut corners to get their lines open as soon as possible. Both had to right those economies within just a few years. In 1851 the LSWR demolished its first timber station in Windsor and replaced it with the imposing mock-Tudor brick and stone edifice that stands to this day. The GWR had also built a wooden station, but in greater style and more solidity so they did not see the need to rebuild it. They did, however, need to replace the timber viaduct. The current brick viaduct was built in 1860.

During the long debates and disputes about bringing the railways to Windsor the points most at issue had been the

The southern wall of the LSWR station is pierced by a lengthy row of these tall doors, each high enough for a mounted man to pass through. They led onto the royal platform and were put here to allow the royal guard to enter and leave the platform in splendid formation.

Never shy of publicity, the LSWR inserted the royal monogram and the date of construction in coloured, glazed bricks into the wall of the royal platform.

121

Built in 1860, the former GWR viaduct still carries the rail lines over the watermeadows to Windsor and Eton Central.

benefits to trade, the impact on Eton College and the effect on the castle and Royal Family. Ironically, the way in which the railways changed Windsor most was never mentioned by either supporters or opponents. And yet within less than a year it had come to take a grip and by 1851 was increasing at an astonishing rate. It was tourism.

Windsor Castle was now within easy reach of a day trip from London. At this time Londoners were not allowed into Buckingham Palace, but the public was allowed in Windsor Castle – or at least into parts of it. The outer bailey and St George's Chapel were always open and the state apartments were open when Queen Victoria was not in residence. Thousands of sightseers poured out of the capital to visit Windsor Castle and gaze at its wonders.

Unknown to the passengers, one of the most astonishing

things about the railway journey, on the GWR at any rate, was the way in which through coaches were transferred from the main line to the branch line. The journey from London was straightforward enough, with a coach being slipped at Slough, then shunted to the branch line. But on the journey to London a bizarre procedure took place. As the train approached Slough, the guard unhitched the rear carriage while the train was moving. The bulk of the train then continued at speed, while the coach freewheeled along, losing speed as it did so. As soon as the train was over the points taking it to the branch platform, the signalman threw the points so that the coach freewheeled to the main line platform ready to be connected to the main line up train. Astonishingly there were never any accidents during the ten years or so that this was done.

In 1897 the GWR finally got round to rebuilding its station at

Something of the splendour of the old GWR can be seen here in the old public ticket office of the Windsor station with its massive wooden fittings.

123

Windsor. It was decided to build three stations next door to each other: a goods station, a public passenger station and a royal station.

The goods station could handle 170 wagons at a time, but was squeezed awkwardly into a corner of the site. Access was down a siding with a steep gradient of 1:45. As a consequence a speed limit of 5 mph was strictly enforced. The public station had five platforms, one a bay, and was constructed of red brick with white stone details. An imposing arch was built over the entrance, which carried the date 1897, a clock and the words 'Great Western Railway' in brass lettering.

The royal station was smaller, but more luxurious. There was only one platform, but it was enormous. The extra width was necessary so that the royal horse-carriage could turn around,

The royal station at the old GWR Windsor station. The stone building to the left is the old royal waiting room. The platform with its arched glass roof was made wide enough for the horses drawing the royal carriage to turn without trouble.

together with the military escort. The entire platform was covered by a glazed roof at the personal request of Queen Victoria who wanted her soldiers to stay dry if they were forced to wait long for her arrival in bad weather.

The new station saw the commencement of through trains from Windsor to Paddington and back. The change was heralded by the unfortunate incidents of two crashes in less than six months, an almost unheard of occurrence on the GWR. The first took place on 23 December 1899 as the 5.47 am from Windsor was crossing the main line to gain the up line at Slough. The mail express from Plymouth was running late through thick fog. It crashed into the side of the Windsor train, slicing it in two before the trains could be brought to a halt. Nobody was seriously hurt, but one passenger lost his Christmas turkey in the wreckage.

The second accident came on 16 June 1900 and was more serious. The 1.05 pm down train to Windsor stopped as usual at Slough at 1.30 pm. As the passengers disembarked, a down express came roaring into the station on the same track as the Windsor train. The driver slammed on the brakes, but did not stop in time. The express ploughed into the rear of the branch

A lone track runs along the old GWR viaduct at Windsor, showing just how much track has been lost along this once busy route.

train, destroying the three rearmost coaches. One coach was thrown into the air and demolished the footbridge above. In all, five people died and another 35 were given hospital treatment.

In both cases it was found that the express driver had missed a signal due to poor visibility. The crashes spurred on work on safety equipment that would lead to experimental work on the Cookham branch line.

In May 1929 the GWR opened a small station at Chalvey Halt, only a mile from Slough Station. It proved to be a commercial failure and was closed just 14 months later.

In 1964 the goods yard at the GWR station was closed due to a lack of business. The yard was converted into a car park. Four years later two of the passenger platforms were closed, followed by a third the next year. The area they once covered is now dedicated to shops and cafés. The two remaining platforms were shortened in the 1970s to allow more space for shops, but the station still provides a frequent service. There are no through trains now, but more than 20 trains run to and from Slough every weekday.

The LSWR station, now known as Windsor and Eton Riverside, has also survived in modified form. The goods yard has been sold for redevelopment as offices, and most of the old buildings have been similarly converted to business use. Here, too, only two platforms remain open, but again a frequent service is still offered.

But the most interesting survivor of the old days at Windsor is the GWR royal

The entrance to Windsor and Eton Riverside station. The former ticket office is now a wine bar, while tickets are purchased through a window that once opened from the porter's office.

Windsor and Eton Riverside, the LSWR station, in the 1920s. Note the number of platforms, plus the engine shed and goods yard to the right.

A similar view today. Only two platforms remain in use, the rest of the station having been demolished and redeveloped as offices. Note the car park to the right that occupies the old goods yard.

The royal waiting room of the LSWR station. A lookout was positioned in the small turret, from whence he could see up the hill to the gates of Windsor Castle and so give a signal when the royal party left the castle. The building has now been converted to be a prestige office suite.

The main entrance to the old GWR station at Windsor. The coat of arms of the company still decorates the top of the structure, but the name has been removed and replaced with the name of the shopping arcade that now fills most of the building.

station. In 1982 British Rail handed over management of the site to Madame Tussaud's, the famous London waxworks. The luxurious royal waiting room, toilet facilities and other amenities were restored to their former glory. The old GWR Achilles class 4-2-2 no 3041 *The Queen* was brought to the platform, together with two restored Victorian royal carriages. The whole complex was opened to the public as the 'Royalty and Empire Exhibition'. It provided a fascinating glimpse into the world of royal railways in the glory days of steam. Sadly, it has now been closed down and the old royal station is now a shopping centre.

9
Lost And Double Lost

The Last Broad Gauge
The Wantage Tramway
The Abingdon Flyer
Steam Train to Wallingford

The tram engine no 5 was formerly the 'Shannon', a locomotive on the Sandy and Potton Railway in Bedfordshire. Its configuration was more obviously that of a railway engine than the others that ran on the Wantage Tramway. The curtain seen on the side of the driver's cab was a rudimentary attempt to provide protection from the rain. This engine is now preserved in full running order at the Didcot Railway Centre.

There are four branch lines that are not only lost in the sense that they no longer exist, but have been doubly lost to Berkshire. Although these lines were built entirely in Berkshire, ran only through Berkshire and closed in Berkshire, their sites are no longer in the county. In 1974 the reorganisation of local government in England saw a large swathe of northern Berkshire transferred to Oxfordshire.

For no good reason other than the whim of a bureaucrat's pen, more than a thousand years of history was wiped away and the sites of these four lines were moved out of their historic home. Since, however, they belonged to Berkshire for the entire time that they operated, these doubly lost lines deserve to be covered here.

The Last Broad Gauge

The most westerly of these branch lines was that which ran to Faringdon. When Brunel was surveying the route of the GWR he decided to run the tracks some three miles south of this bustling market town with its charming stone houses and impressive church. He did install a station named Faringdon Road where the line crossed what is now the A417. The designation 'Road' was often used by the GWR to indicate that the station was the nearest to a particular place without actually being in it.

The good citizens of Faringdon did not care for being bypassed in this way and in 1860 sponsored an Act of Parliament that gave permission for the Faringdon Railway Company to build a 3½ mile line from the town to the GWR main line a short distance to the west of the Faringdon Road station. The company came to an agreement with the GWR so that the larger company would operate the branch line. A passenger train would run a shuttle service, resting overnight in an engine shed at Faringdon, while freight services would see main line trains slip trucks into a siding where they could be picked up by the branch locomotive. This necessitated the branch line being built on the broad gauge so that trucks from the GWR could run over the lines.

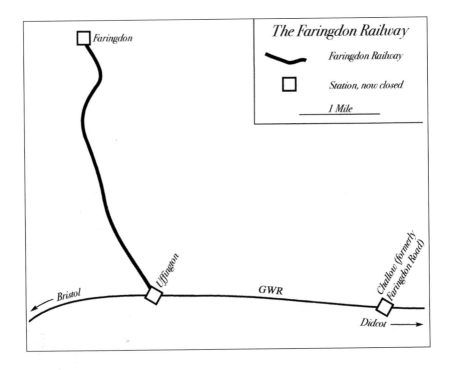

It was decided that the new main line junction station would go by the name of Uffington, while the old Faringdon Road would become Challow, as those were the nearest villages to the two stops.

Construction got under way in March 1861 with an engineer and contractor from Wales in charge. Almost at once two problems caused work to cease. The first was that the East Gloucestershire Railway put a Bill before Parliament seeking permission for a line from Faringdon west to Cheltenham. This would have required changes to the layout of the Faringdon line, so work was halted until such time as the Bill could become an Act. In the event the Bill was voted down.

Work could not restart as the company had failed to raise enough money to complete the line. The crisis was solved when Oriel College, Oxford, which owned much of the land to be

Uffington station, looking towards Bristol. A coal train passes through on the up line in the 1950s. The engine has halted beside the wooden signal box, behind which can be seen the chimneys of the station buildings proper. The branch line to Faringdon can be seen curving away to the right.

A London to Bristol express thunders today through what was once Uffington station. This photo was taken from the bridge visible at the rear of the older photo. Both platforms have been removed, as has the signal box. The station itself has now been converted to a private house and is just out of shot to the left. The brick building visible beyond the train is the former Junction Hotel, now also a private house.

133

crossed, agreed to be paid in the form of shares rather than cash. Work began again in March 1863 and the line was finished by April 1864.

The Board of Trade inspector arrived and promptly failed the line as unsafe for public use. He considered that the signalling equipment was inadequate. Another defect was that the level crossing that allowed the farmer at Moor Mill Farm to drive his cattle to pasture did not have locking gates. This meant that there was nothing to stop the cattle wandering off down the line, creating an obvious hazard to trains. Just such an incident would later feature in the popular *Thomas the Tank Engine* books by the Rev W.A. Awdry.

The contractor, Mr Lewis of Carmarthen, rectified the faults in time for the official opening on 1 June 1864. The town council of Faringdon declared the day to be a public holiday – local government having such powers in those days – and the town celebrated with special trains and a small fair.

At first there were four passenger trains in each direction from Monday to Saturday with three on a Sunday. The locomotive hauled goods trucks in between the 10 minute passenger runs. The opening of the line boosted business for Faringdon so much that the number of passenger trains soon increased to six daily. As an indication of the growth in trade, it should be noted that the town had previously dispatched six milk churns daily on a cart to Faringdon Road station, but within a decade was sending out 24 by direct train.

The line was popular and profitable, but was not making so much money that the directors felt justified in spending the extra needed to convert the line from broad gauge to the increasingly popular standard gauge. Even when the GWR main line was converted to take both standard and broad gauge trucks, the Faringdon Railway Company refused to change. It was this lack of money that led to the Faringdon Railway being the last broad gauge line operating in England, outside of Devon.

Eventually, in 1878, the GWR presented the Faringdon Railway Company with an ultimatum. Unless the line was converted, the GWR would no longer be able to handle freight on the line. Already goods arriving by standard gauge trucks

A panoramic view of Faringdon taken in about 1912 looking towards the north. (Courtesy of Lens of Sutton)

were being offloaded at Challow and taken to Faringdon by road, at some cost and inconvenience. The GWR offered to carry out the work at a discount price of just £102, so the directors of the smaller company agreed. On 26 July 1878 the branch line was closed and large numbers of GWR workmen swarmed over the area. Within 48 hours the change had been made and the Faringdon Railway reopened as a standard gauge line.

The smaller company had always been reliant on the GWR, and the change in gauge seems to have made it more so. In 1886 the GWR bought the Faringdon Railway Company. The change in ownership made no real difference to the operation of the line, which continued much as before. It was not until after the Second World War that changing times caught up with the Faringdon branch line. A regular bus service was begun, linking the town with Swindon and Oxford, causing passenger numbers on the train to fall off. The problem was not so much cost as the fact that the shuttle train deposited passengers at Uffington, where they then had to wait around for a connecting train while the bus ran direct. By the end of 1951 it was clear that the passenger train was no longer paying its way, so the service was closed on 29 December.

Freight traffic continued to be profitable, relying especially on the agricultural produce of the area. However, even milk and cattle began to be moved more by road than on the rails. On 1 July 1963 the freight service to Faringdon was halted.

135

Thereafter the branch line survived for a while as a useful siding off the main line, and the Royal Train was parked there more than once. Eventually even this use became redundant and the rails were lifted.

No longer able to pay their way, both Uffington and Challow stations closed. Faringdon no longer has a link to the railway network. At both places some buildings remain, but they are now used by businesses independent of the railways, while the platforms have been dismantled.

Of the Faringdon line itself little remains. In Faringdon most of the station was demolished to make way for warehouses and industrial buildings. Only the unusual passenger station survives, now serving as a nursery school. The route of the line running out of the town is now covered by the A417, as it heads south-east to join a modern bypass around the town. Beyond the

Seen from the north, townside, the unusual construction of the passenger station buildings at Faringdon can be clearly seen. The double roof was unique on the GWR, while the double chimney drew smoke from the fires in the waiting room and stationmaster's office. The public courtyard was to the left, and the platform to the right. A fence dividing the two formerly ran from the centre of the building towards the photographer. A new building has been built to the right and the once open canopy walled in to provide an extra room.

The old passenger station at Faringdon, as it is today. This is the front of the station, which fronted onto a small yard – and this opened through ornamental gates into the town. The doorway gave access to a ticket office.

The ornamental gates that once gave access to Faringdon station from the town. They could be locked at night to secure the station.

Faringdon station is now occupied by a popular nursery school.

Photographed in 1960 this shot of Uffington shows the main lines on the left with the branch line to the right. The small building is the signal cabin. (Courtesy of Lens of Sutton)

bypass, the line of the railway can be traced as it enters a short cutting, but it then crosses open land where all trace of the line has vanished.

At the Uffington end of the old line the site of the troublesome level crossing has vanished. The location of the junction with the main line can be identified, but there is not much left of the branch line. The old main line station is now a private house, though the platforms, signal box and other ancillary buildings have all been demolished. The Junction Hotel is, likewise, a private house.

The Faringdon Railway is lost indeed.

The Wantage Tramway

A few miles east of Faringdon, Wantage had also been bypassed by the GWR main line. Unlike the citizens of Faringdon, however, those of Wantage were not too bothered by the fact. When the idea of a branch line was suggested in 1866 the plan collapsed because so few people in the town were willing to invest in it.

By 1873 things had changed. The key factor was the passing by Parliament of the Tramways Act. This allowed light rail lines to be laid on public roads to carry passenger and freight trams. Tramlines were cheaper to build and operate than were railways and a group of Wantage businessmen believed that they could make a line pay. On 10 November 1873 the Wantage Tramway Company was established and by August 1875 the line had been completed. It opened for business in October.

One of the company's first acts was to buy out Mr Nunney, who operated a horse bus between the town and the GWR's Wantage Road station. Mr Nunney was paid £100 for his horse, his bus and for the freight and postal contracts that he operated. The horse was put to work pulling the company's sole tramcar until such time as steam stock could be purchased.

The line began in the GWR goods yard at Wantage Road, although the company was to remain entirely independent of the GWR throughout its life. The rails then ran down the east

The site of the stop at Grove as it is today. The stream passes under the road at the spot where the concrete pillars can be seen on the left. When the tramway ran here the road was only half as wide as it is now with the tramway running along its eastern edge, approximately where the central white lines are now.

side of what is now the A338 towards Wantage. At Grove the tracks diverged from the road to cross a specially built 38 feet long bridge over the Wiltshire and Berkshire Canal before rejoining the road south of the bridge. Just north of Wantage, the line crossed a stream, then divided in two. The eastern spur ran uphill into the town centre where the Upper Yard had a small platform for passengers and a shed to store the rolling stock. The western spur ran along the streamside to Clark's Flour Mill, where the Lower Yard was built.

It was not until 1 August 1876 that steam trams began to run along the line in the shape of a tramcar with its boiler and machinery located inside the car itself. The machine could carry 54 passengers. In March the following year a steam tram engine, which hauled tramcars, arrived. This was found to be too weak

140

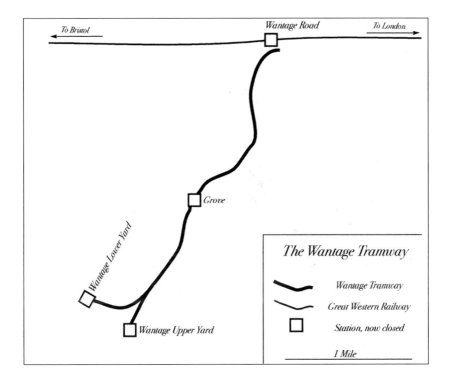

to haul the goods trucks, so the search for a replacement began. In May 1878 the Wantage Tramway bought a small 0-4-0WT locomotive named *Shannon* second-hand from the London and North Western Railway. The little engine was renamed as the rather prosaic *Wantage No 5* and put to work. It proved to be an outstanding success. Not only could it haul the heavy flour trucks from Clark's Mill, but it was so efficient that it halved the coal consumption per mile.

Thereafter the Wantage Tramway purchased a wide variety of small engines and tramcars, most of them second-hand. The eclectic mix of styles and patterns was a notable feature of the line. Only the uniform green paint scheme showed any sign of company style.

The fortunes of the Wantage Tramway peaked in 1905. That

141

Wantage Tramway engine no 6 was bought in 1888 and remained in operation until the First World War. It is seen here in 1889 at Upper Yard about to haul a tramcar to Wantage Road station to link up with an expected GWR passenger train.

year the company used four engines to move a daily average of over 150 passengers and 14 goods wagons. It was enough to turn a handsome profit and to pay a good dividend to shareholders. It could not last. In October 1924 a bus company began a rival service from the Wantage Road GWR station to Wantage. Within a year the tramway cancelled its passenger service, and sold two of the engines.

The goods service continued to make a profit, though it was not as great as before. In the end it was circumstances beyond the control of the tramway that caused its demise. In 1943 the US Army established a vast base at Grove in preparation for D-Day. Thousands of trucks, tanks and armoured vehicles moved in and out of the camp over the following two years. Although they were supposed to stay on the road, many ran over the tram

Taken in the later 1950s, this picture of Wantage Road shows the footbridge and various buildings that then stood on this station. The main lines remain, but nearly everything else has now vanished. (Courtesy of Lens of Sutton)

tracks, causing considerable damage.

When the war ended in 1945, the Tramway Company directors ordered a survey of their line. The surveyor found the line so badly degraded that he recommended a complete rebuilding. The company could not afford such an expense on the basis of the freight profits, so the line was closed. On 25 April 1946 the rolling stock was auctioned off, while the lifted tracks went to scrap. The proceeds of the sale were distributed to shareholders and the company wound up.

There is, today, almost nothing left of the Wantage Tramway. The route of the tracks has been engulfed by the widening of the A338 to such an extent that it is not even possible to see where they once ran. The bridge over the canal was thoroughly dismantled and no traces of it remain. Both Upper and Lower Yards have been redeveloped. But the Wantage Tramway is not entirely lost. Engine *Wantage No 5*, the former *Shannon*, was bought by the GWR in 1946. When British Rail abandoned steam, the engine was given to the Great Western Society's

The former site of the Wantage Road station photographed in 2006. The buildings to the left occupy the site of the down platform, while the open ground to the right is where the freight yard once stood. The northern end of the tramway lay just in front of the trees to the right of the picture.

working museum at Didcot. It is there still, periodically puffing away to pull tourists and enthusiasts up and down a short branch line.

The Abingdon Flyer

To the north-east of Wantage lies the town of Abingdon. In 1844 the Oxford and Great Western Union Railway had built a line from Oxford to link up with the GWR at Didcot. Thomas Duffield, the MP for Abingdon, together with the three largest landowners in the area did not want the railway in Abingdon, so the new line bypassed the town to the east.

By 1854, however, the town council had become concerned that they were missing out on the rapid industrialisation and increasing prosperity of towns that were on the railway. They managed to overcome the objections of the landowners and in 1855 successfully sponsored the Abingdon Railway Act through Parliament. This approved a plan by the specially formed Abingdon Railway Company to build a broad gauge line from Abingdon to join the main line, now owned by the GWR. In order to drum up support for the railway and the sale of its shares, the directors referred to the proposed line by the rather ambitious title of the 'Abingdon Flyer', a name borrowed from the horse-drawn coach service that had linked the town to London some 40 years earlier.

In the event shares sold well and work began before the end of the year. The contractor chosen was a rather unlikely character by the name of George Furness. He owned a brick factory in Willesden and had won a contract to dredge and improve dock facilities in the harbour at La Spezia, in Italy, but was quite unknown in the railway business. Nevertheless, he did his work well. Furness hired 120 navvies and completed the two mile broad gauge line, together with a station in Abingdon and a rather rudimentary platform stop on the main line that was named Abingdon Junction. Work was completed promptly by June 1856 and a grand celebratory dinner was held at County Hall. The navvies were given a hearty supper down the road at the Rising Sun.

The line was an immediate success, both in terms of popularity and profitability. The services were run by the GWR, using GWR staff, locomotives and rolling stock. As with so many branch lines off the GWR serving sizeable towns it was coal that was the main cargo. Homes and businesses both burned enormous quantities of coal to provide heat and power, so the demand was high. In 1872 Abingdon Railway chose to convert to standard gauge, the one used by most branch lines off the GWR at this time. The work was completed in a single day: 26 November.

In 1873 the open platforms of Abingdon Junction were abandoned. The branch line was extended north alongside the main line to reach the village of Radley, where a new station was built. The new stop had the advantages over the old of not only having road access, but also being given proper station

A Dean 4-4-2 races through the Abingdon Road Halt in 1912. Passengers could change here to take the branch line into Abingdon itself. (Courtesy of Lens of Sutton)

buildings and shelters over the platforms. Business boomed afresh. The line was so profitable that in 1904 the GWR offered to pay £20 for every £10 share. The shareholders agreed and the Abingdon Railway Company was bought out by the GWR.

The change of ownership made little difference to the operation of the branch line. The passenger trains were worked by a tank engine, which shuttled back and forth between Radley and Abingdon, stopping overnight in the train shed at Abingdon. Although the engines changed from time to time, they tended to be of the 517 class or similar. The passenger trains consisted of four coaches, which by 1900 were of the four-wheel GWR style. In the same year the passenger train was running back and forth 16 times each day, taking a scheduled five minutes for the run each way.

Goods trains were worked by whichever engine was pulling them along the main line, so there was no standard vehicle running on the line. In addition to the profitable coal trade, the line also carried large quantities of animal skins to the big tannery in the town and, on Mondays, shipped out significant

The GWR 0-4-2 tank no 1446 hauling a freight train out of Abingdon. Although the photo is undated, it is probably from the later 1950s when trains of this type became more numerous on the line, following the closure of the train shed at Abingdon. The date is confirmed by the driver's hairstyle.

numbers of cattle from the livestock market. By 1932 the creation of the MG car works in the town meant that the transport of cars had become the main freight business of the line.

After the Second World War the fortunes of the Abingdon Flyer began to decline. A regular and frequent bus service was begun between the town and Oxford, which took away most of the passenger traffic. By 1958 the passenger train had been removed and replaced by a single unit diesel motor unit (DMU). On 9 September 1963 this ran for the last time and passenger services ceased on the Abingdon line.

Freight traffic, however, remained highly profitable. This was largely due to the MG works, which continued to send its cars out by rail. In May 1980 the MG works was closed down, production being moved to the main British Leyland works. A lone, weekly goods train continued to run for another four years, but nothing turned up to provide extra traffic, so this was discontinued in March 1984. Thereafter the flat, straight line proved to be useful for training drivers and other staff, so it was kept on by British Rail for several more years.

Eventually the cost of maintenance outweighed the benefits and the Abingdon line was finally closed down completely.

Today there is very little left to show there was ever a rail line here. The flat land did not demand any embankments or cuttings that would have to remain after the rails were lifted. The station in Abingdon has been demolished completely and the prime town centre site sold off for development. Radley station remains, but only just. The original buildings were demolished when the branch line was closed, to be replaced by brick-built shelters.

Steam Train to Wallingford

South-east of Abingdon, the good citizens of Wallingford had

The 14XX class 0-4-2 tank engine no 1407 waits at Wallingford beside the water tank that dominated the station. This photo was taken in about 1960. (Courtesy of Lens of Sutton)

The Cholsey and Moulsford station photographed in about 1960. The line on the right of the picture is the bay platform, running off to the north before it swings to the right to head for Wallingford. (Courtesy of Lens of Sutton)

been railway enthusiasts from the moment the GWR was first proposed. They were deeply disappointed when the main line passed three miles west of their town and were particularly annoyed in 1866 when the Wallingford Road station built to serve the town was renamed Moulsford. Within six months, protests from the town got the station's name changed back to Wallingford Road.

This was not enough for the people of Wallingford. When the GWR steadfastly refused to add a branch line, the town decided to build one for itself. In 1864 the Wallingford and Watlington Railway Company gained an Act of Parliament authorising it to construct a line from the GWR main line near Cholsey to Watlington. The company opted to build on the standard gauge, so the line could not share rolling stock with broad gauge GWR. Instead the branch line had a bay platform at the old Wallingford Road station, now renamed Moulsford once again.

The Wallingford and Watlington Railway Company was able

The original station nameplate from Wallingford, now restored and on show at the new Wallingford station just outside of town. (Courtesy of the Cholsey and Wallingford Railway Preservation Society)

to raise only enough money to build the line from Cholsey as far as Wallingford. The cost of bridging the Thames proved to be beyond the abilities of the brokers to sell shares, so Watlington remained without its railway. Nevertheless, the company directors were jubilant as they rode the first train from Moulsford to Wallingford on 2 July 1866.

The line was 3¼ miles long, running over almost flat ground other than a short descent of 1:202 into Wallingford itself. Apart from a sharp corner at the Moulsford end, the line was almost completely straight. The station at Wallingford had a single platform able to accommodate four coaches together with a small, but neat station building of red brick with white stone cornicing. Adjacent to the station was a surprisingly large goods yard with six roads. The main business was bringing coal into the nearby gasworks and coke factory and taking goods away from the Co-op's massive dairy and egg handling works that stood in the town.

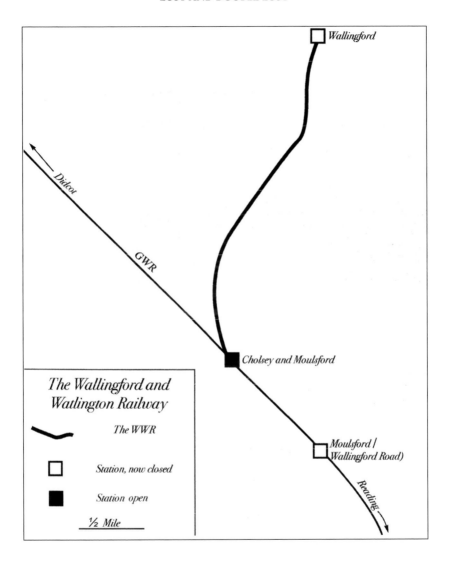

The Wallingford and
Watlington Railway

The WWR

☐ Station, now closed

■ Station open

½ Mile

In 1872 the directors of the Wallingford and Watlington Railway Company finally gave up all hope of raising enough money to bridge the Thames and extend their line to Watlington. Instead they sold up to the GWR, which took over ownership of

A scale model of Wallingford station as it was in the 1930s. All the buildings shown here, including the church and school, were demolished when the station was closed and the site sold for redevelopment in the 1960s. (Courtesy of the Cholsey and Wallingford Railway Preservation Society).

152

the line. The GWR ran a wide variety of tank engines on the line throughout its life. At first these locomotives were housed overnight at the engine shed in Wallingford, but after 1956 a new engine was sent each day from the depot at Didcot, the shed having been closed to save money.

In 1892 the main line was transformed by being widened from two to four tracks. The GWR took advantage of the change to close down Mouslford station and to replace it with an entirely new station, named Cholsey and Moulsford. The new station was located where the branch line diverged from the main line.

It was during the 1920s that the branch line was busiest. Each day 18 passenger trains ran each way, while an average of 45 goods trucks were worked along the line. On Sundays there was only one train, a milk special hauling fresh milk out of the Co-op dairy. The line had an operating profit of around 17%, though most of this was swallowed up in provision for maintenance.

As with so many other branch lines, the passenger and freight traffic gradually moved over to road transport. The process accelerated in the 1950s to such an extent that the last passenger train ran to Wallingford on 15 June 1959. By 1965 there was only one freight customer left: the huge British Maltsters Ltd malt mill that stood on the outskirts of the town. The line was kept open for the sole purpose of bringing grain in and malt out of this works, all other services being suspended. The line between the mill and town was lifted, the station demolished and the site sold off for housing development.

In the spring of 1981 a regular inspection showed that the points at Cholsey needed replacing and that the track would soon need attention. Neither British Rail nor British Maltsters was willing to pay the bill, so the line was doomed. Before the line was finally closed on 31 May 1981 British Rail ran a special, dubbed by the local press 'The Wallingford Wake', pulled by a diesel unit for the benefit of railway enthusiasts.

After the special left the malt factory sidings, the line was shut down. The Wallingford branch seemed doomed to become just another of the lost railways of Berkshire.

And so it might have been had it not been for a dedicated band of local enthusiasts. Although the points at Cholsey were

153

The handwritten note that was pinned to the noticeboard at Cholsey station in May 1959. It gives details of the new bus services that were being introduced to replace the passenger trains that would no longer run to Wallingford.

removed, the track was retained. In 1982 the Cholsey and Wallingford Railway Preservation Society was formed. Funds were raised, engines and rolling stock acquired and the track leased at a peppercorn rent. Aided by supporters and friends, the Society runs steam and diesel trains from Cholsey and Wallingford between May and September. October sees special Hallowe'en Trains running on the line, while Santa Specials run in the lead up to Christmas and there is a special Carol Train just before Christmas itself.

The former maltings sidings have been converted into a station with a gift shop, railway museum and a diorama of the

A view of the controls of the 0-4-0 saddletank engine 'Thames', no 2351, built by Barclays in 1951. Tank engines similar to this ran on the GWR branch lines. This engine is now preserved in full running order at Wallingford. (With thanks to the Cholsey and Wallingford Railway Preservation Society)

The 'Thames' sits at the end of the line in Wallingford.

Remnants of Brunel's broad gauge vision can be found in surprising places. This broad gauge carriage spent several decades being used as a chicken shed on a farm in Wales. It is now resting in Wallingford where it serves as a café offering the most delicious home-made meals. (Courtesy of the Cholsey and Wallingford Railway Preservation Society)

station as it was in 1930. Although the line never operated on the broad gauge that began the story of the railways in Berkshire, the Society has acquired an old broad gauge passenger carriage. It sits beside the lines and has been converted into a café that serves what must be the best fried breakfast in the area.

So, some of the branch lines of Berkshire are gone, leaving behind only converted buildings, overgrown embankments and fond memories. But when steam is up at Wallingford and bacon sizzles in the pan it can almost seem as if the Lost Railways of Berkshire have been found once again.

INDEX